I LOOKED FOR A MAN AND FOUND ONE

LORENE MILEY

I LOOKED FOR A MAN . . .
AND FOUND ONE
© Copyright 1983
Randall House Publications
Nashville, Tennessee
ISBN 0-89265-088-5

Printed in the United States of America

TO

Larry

Who once aspired to be
a medical missionary
"just like my dad."

" . . . How beautiful are the feet
of them that preach the gospel
of peace . . . " (Romans 10:15).

Contents

Preface

This book is not an anthropological discourse of the Lobi tribe of West Africa, although I hope you will become acquainted with some of these dark children of the sun and sense their capacity for love, their sorrow in paganism, and their innate longing and searching after the God who loved and created them.

It is not primarily an historical account of our near-two decades in Ivory Coast, although we've striven for accuracy as dates were interwoven with facts and places. Admittedly, these facts are tinged with emotion.

This book is an effort to tell the story of a man whom God led to a mission field. A missionary who not only went with his feet to publish the gospel of love, but at the same time, a doctor who offered his hands in an effort to demonstrate that love.

The gospels clearly illustrate that no two reporters view a scene the same way. Had other participants this same opportunity, they might describe my man differently. In life there is no instant replay whereby we may evaluate life's fleeting episodes. We have only our faulty words and memories. Facts remain, but impressions and interpretations give various kaleidoscopic versions to the whole image.

Come now with me to Lobi Land for a replay of life in slow motion. This is the doctor as I know him and the scenes as I felt them.

Lorene Miley
June, 1983
Nashville, Tn.

Introduction

This book is the story of a man who found that success is obeying God.

The author writes from an intimate, firsthand, on-the-field relationship with her missionary-doctor husband.

Lorene Miley successfully thrusts her bifocals on our eyes. She allows us to see up close the compelling convictions, forged from God's Word and the furnace of Christian experience, which propelled LaVerne Miley from Bible College, to seminary, medical school, and the mission field.

She permits us to share the heartbeat experiences of complete trust in God for provision and guidance through the educational process. The guiding, providing hand of God is in clear focus throughout.

The sufficiency of God proved more than adequate through language study in France and Africa, clinic establishment at Doropo, protection from Satanic forces, and nature's serpents.

The reality of the Psalmist's prayer has been their reward. "Let thy work appear unto thy servants, and thy glory unto their children. And let the beauty of the LORD our God be upon us: and establish thou the work of our hands upon us; yea, the work of our hands establish thou it" (Psalm 90:16, 17).

H. D. Harrison

PART I
A BRIEF LOOK AT
LOBI LAND

Come now with me to this country,
To the land you've only heard of.
Hear its sounds and smell the odors,
Taste the dust and sense the danger.
Watch the people steeped in magic,
See their faces, sad and hopeless.
Learn their names and stop to listen
To their silent cry, "Come help us."
    These my people--they're called Lobis.

-1-

The Epidemic

Lobi Land 1962

The harmattan winds began earlier and lasted longer than usual that dry season of 1962. Originating in the dust bowl of the African Saharas, they swept violently down from the north until Lobi Land smothered in a thick fog of dust, sand, and microscopic particles of death.

Recent fires had ravaged the land, obliterating every trace of rainy season growth. Majestic grain stalks and hardy peanut and yam runners were reduced to layers of ashes blanketing the splotchy plots of land. The odor of burning wood hung heavy in the air. The land lay parched and smoldering with tiny ripples of heat spiraling from the blackened stubble. Occasionally a column of air would strike the ground, scoop up a mass of dirt and debris and explode upward, then like a swirling top, zigzag up and down like a mischievous boy capering across the downs. Finally many minutes later and several miles from its origin, the twister peters out, casting its accumulation aside like unwanted refuse.

These germ-laden whirlwinds became nature's rapid transit system transporting the deadly germs of infection from village to village. In such breeding ground spinal meningitis erupted and thrived so heartily until Lobi Land found herself in the grips of an epidemic which threatened to touch virtually every village in its path.

Two women sat silently in the small courtyard of the Old Chief's compound. The younger, probably still a teenager, sat propped against her small circular hut, her legs outstretched before her. A feverish babe tossed fitfully at her bare breast.

Her sister wife, probably not more than two or three years

11

older, rose to a standing position, stretched leisurely, and glided toward a blackened pot posed on three large stones in the center of the courtyard. Stooping gracefully with straightened back, she removed an extended stick and wakened the smoldering fire under the pot. She added another stick, reached for the wooden mallet, and began to stir the simmering millet mush.

"If you ask me," Afia broke the silence, raised the wooden spoon in mid-air and pointed to the thrashing child of the girl-mother. "If you ask me," she repeated, "I'd say that Second One of yours has the mark of death on her."

"No!" the younger screams, more from fear than anger. "If you ask me, I'd say you put a curse on her. You did, you did! Just because you aren't woman enough to have a living child, you want to kill this one of mine. You're jealous, that's what! You were jealous of my Sie and now you're jealous of my Eri." She hugged the child closer to her and took up a chant. "Jealous, jealous, jealous."

Manakir had struck an exposed nerve. Afia *was* childless. Twice she had suffered the birthing pains—once a man child and once a girl baby—but neither had lived past the second day.

"Jealous you say?" Afia struck back. "Of what? Of that cadaver there? Ha!"

The wounded mother searched for a weapon to throw at that pestering sister wife, but before she could locate something in arm's reach, Afia had grabbed her water basin and headed for the river two miles away. Unlike Hannah of old, she had no one with whom to share her heartache.

The girl baby arched her tiny back and mewed her discomfort. The girl mother rubbed a calloused hand over the feverish bottom, then sighed helplessly. "Oh, well . . . . "

In another part of the compound, the Old Chief, patriarch of his extended family, stretched lazily the length of his bamboo chaise-lounge. He reached into his goat skin bag and removed a small container of snuff. Tapping the packed contents on his bony knee cap, he began his ritual, slowly, deliberately, as though to delay the more urgent matter consuming his thoughts.

A feeling of sleep lay on the world. A bumblebee buzzed noisily in his ear and he shooed it away with his cow tail flychaser.

Bielkhiri judged it to be an hour or two before nightfall. The dying wind lingered only as a stifling oppression of red powder, distilling fear into his heart as well as the more than 20,000 souls who inhabited this border area separating Ivory Coast from Upper Volta. With the darkness, he knew the elders would come. What could they hope to do to stay this powerful hand of death stretched out over their land? Only today the drums beat out news of the latest victims.

Bielkhiri leaned back and closed his eyes. This fetish they served ruled as a relentless taskmaster, unmerciful and cruel. He feared this invisible dictator of his existence, but that didn't mean he respected him.

Fratonna, eldest wife of the Old Chief, sat on the ground next to her husband, her legs stretched straight before her. The years had sharply grooved her frail body. Freshly shaven head and naked except for a scanty cloth wrapped about her hips and tucked between her legs, she looked like a dark heap of skin and bones. Discs about the size of half-dollars caused her lips to protrude duck-bill fashion. The other three wives pounded and stirred in another part of the courtyard, but the Old One having come to this man's house more than 30 years before and borne him a half a dozen children grown to adulthood, basked in her retirement from physical servitude.

The two pondered their thoughts in silence, oblivious to the courtyard activity. Mantona and Lonapirina, feuding as usual, prepared the millet mush. Cin'Tin, hardly more than a child herself, strapped a crying baby to her bare back with a ragged cloth, rhythmically rocking the child to quietness. Other children crept close in anticipation, the smell of the bubbling grain almost more than they could contain. Even though born in the compound of the chief, not every day did the rumbling of their stomachs promise to be stilled.

In such manner twilight captured the land.

"Eat, my husband," spoke Mantona, the second one, as she knelt on the ground beside the Old Chief and placed a calabash into his idle hands. "Eat," she repeated. "Strength to your spirit it will give."

"Oo," grunted Bielkhiri in pleasure and dipped bare fingers

in the thickened gruel. After his stomach was satisfied, his spirit would be free to think.

The Old Chief did not leave his chair until he had eaten his fill of the thick, pink mush. Now he raised to his full six-foot height, then slumped into his natural hunched poise. The average life span in this country is a mere 45, and he had already passed 40. Deeply etched facial lines competed with the faint tribal cat-like markings fanning from the corners of his eyes. His stooped posture came not so much with age but from a huge football size inguinal hernia, a burden laid on him with the coming of his manhood. His super short mini-dress and drawstring shorts fashioned from durable native cloth did little to hide this medical problem common to the black race.

As Bielkhiri was not impressive as a man, neither was his compound an imposing one. Four round, thatch-roofed huts, one for each of his wives, fanned from the small courtyard. A smaller one stored his grain and, most important of all, his fetish house which sheltered his balafon, drums, images, and other objects of worship. Adjoining his quarters but possessing private courtyards sprawled the dwellings of three of his married sons and their families. The children from these unions were claimed as his own. Not much to boast of, he thought. Djimpate's Afia had buried her only two, and now his First One's girl baby was ailing.

Having received the chief's mantle from his father, Bielkhiri would in turn pass it on to his oldest son, Djimpate. By right of his paternal position, Bielkhiri offered sacrifices and entreated the fetish for his people, yet the spiritual power of the tribe rested in hands other than his.

He crinkled his eyes and peered through the dust. The primrose sky blended with the barren landscape and obscured the village three quarters of a mile to the north. A hundred yards away and separated by dormant fields, similar compounds dotted a radius about three miles in diameter toward the south.

Bielkhiri waited as the curtain of darkness fell. He didn't wait long.

"Mi foure," greeted the first visitor.

"Oo, mi toure," Bielkhiri responded. The presence of Lealte, the medicine man, filled the courtyard.

Dreams, divination, medicine, sorcery, witchcraft, and taboos all form a communication network between the world of power and the faith of the Lobi people. Although Lealte's treatments often involved a lot of hokus-pokus, it could not be denied he rated high in the knowledge of herbalogy. He boasted a firsthand acquaintance with virtually every plant in his domain. No, he hadn't developed uses for them all, yet he constantly experimented. With neither book, instrument, nor instructor, this feat in itself seemed most admirable.

The two dispensed with formalities and sat in silence. Soon, "Caw-Caw" and the slap of the hands announced Djorfite's arrival. The fame of this spiritual leader rested in his trumpet, a relic from military days in the French army. Often the insistent sound of this horn punctuated the stillness of the night as Djorfite called the wandering spirits to himself.

Djorfite exuded demonic power, reputed to be an expert in ventriloquism, hypnosis, and sleight of hand tricks. A mean, violent man when drunk—much of the time—this dirty little bandy-legged man could hardly rate a second look when sober.

Dabolo, the nearest neighbor, arrived last. Dabolo was not his real name, but rather a tribal name of homage that an earlier missionary had bestowed on him out of respect for his age and tribal position. An artisan in wood and metal, this meningitis epidemic produced a profitable little business for him. He amassed quite a horde of unusual pods, buttons, old coins, and shells. These with other forged metals and carved wood were fashioned into charms. Properly bargained for and spirit-imparted, these amulets were fastened on strings and tied around necks, ankles, on baby baskets or attached to hip beads. Parents literally paid their last piece of money, their cache of cowrie shells, or even chased down their last chicken to obtain this protection. What else could they do? Could they stand by and watch their own flesh and blood drop off like flies?

Dabolo offered them something to clutch in their hands but absolutely nothing to hide in their hearts.

Thus it was. These reponsible leaders and clan representatives filed into the Old Chief's courtyard for this urgent meeting with the only God they knew existed—the fetish.

15

"It would seem Thangba is angered with us," the Old Chief began.

"Thangba," Dabolo repeated the name for creator God with reverence. "What does He care anyway?" At rare moments he caught a fleeting glimpse of this Supreme Being as he explored the creation's nooks and crannies, but he could never quite put flesh on it. Unable to do so, he devised his own method of worship. Those amulets, formed as birds and animals and snakes and men, possessed a power able to perform far more than that elusive Thangba out there somewhere.

Men spat, one snored, the night wore on. Somewhere a rooster crowed.

After a long period of silence, Mantona stepped behind her husband, placed a huge gourd of millet beer in his lap, and then disappeared into the darkness. The highly intoxicating drink made its rounds again and again until tongues were loosened and heads light.

Sharp claps and a low intonation from the Old Chief filled the smoke-filled room. The men crouched on the packed mud floor immediately straightened to stiff attention. Picking up the chant, voices blended as one to invoke the only force they were able to contact.

A rush of air swept through their midst. A hush settled over the men, even the air hung suspended. With a flick of the wrist, Bielkhiri removed the knife from his waist band and tipped the overturned gourd behind him releasing a sleeping chicken. Before the first squawk of surprise, the blade slit the throat and the chicken thrashed to and fro before them, the warm blood flecking the clothing of the mute men.

This way, then that. Which way would it lie in death? If it breathed its last breath on the back, favor smiled on them. It would mean the fetish had accepted their efforts. He would still this epidemic of death ravaging their land. Alas, should it settle on the side, it could only mean they were helpless. They could do nothing.

Death came slowly to the writhing sacrifice. A sigh of relief sprang from waiting men as the chicken settled on the back. One second passed, two and three. With a horrible last fling, the

16

chicken leaped in the air, flopped with wings outspread, and finally, and irrevocably, lay mute and lifeless on the breast. The fetish had not accepted their sacrifice.

Despair and hopelessness framed the faces of the elders. Oh, well, sometimes it works and sometimes it doesn't. Any fool knew these sacrifices weren't 100% successful, but the fact that they worked sometimes was force enough to depend on it.

Suddenly the night came alive with the wail of many voices lifted in the death wail. The call of the katydid and the pleas of the bush baby hushed to the vibrating wails of the mourners and the warming up strains of the balafon. Trained ears strained toward the familiar scenario. They didn't wait long. The exploding blast of powder from a homemade gun scared off the initial spirits as one somewhere began her journey to the City of the Dead.

Before the first streak of dawn, men rose on weary knees, stretched widely, and prepared to leave. A statement from the Old Chief alerted them to attention.

"It is said that the white man living across the way is a medicine man. It is said he can make sick people live in good health again. It is only said. No one knows."

The seed dropped in fertile soil. Before many hours passed, it would blossom to fruition.

"Yes, I've seen that white man," thought Djorfite and quickly identified him with other white men he had known. When Ivory Coast was still a French colony, the government built roads and buildings with enforced labor. Djorfite carried scars across his back to testify that, in his opinion, "All white men were cruel and violent."

"They're so nosy," added Dabolo, voicing his observation. "Always carrying those little boxes to capture the souls of our people. Surely that must be why they are so rich. Don't they demand payment just to look at them?"

"And what about that white man just three years previously? Why did he sneak in on those initiation rites when he had been warned to stay away? Surely he had been up to no good. Why, they had had no choice but to fill him with their poisoned arrows."

The knowledge of a white medicine man living in their midst produced perplexing and conflicting opinions. Had he come to

17

merely heal their sick? Would he enforce them to labor, do away with their customs, intrude into their manner of living or--could it even be--eat their children?

Dabolo's decision to go see the white doctor was born neither from curiosity nor competitive interest, but from an urgent need. On arrival at his compound a few minutes later, he found his only daughter, just three years old, delirious with fever. So his potent charms had not protected his own flesh from the deadly germs. He wrapped her unconscious frame in his arms and strode across the road to the white doctor's house. His existence had offered a wide range of experiences in pain and suffering, but almost nothing in the realm of hope. Little did he know that the God his ancestors had cast aside was about to be revealed in a way he could not fail to recognize.

Dabolo was not alone on that memorable morning. The okay signal seemed to have alerted other villages as well. The sick were brought on homemade stretchers, the bodies wrapped in cloths and suspended on bamboo poles borne by two. Some were carried in arms. Others were brought on bicycles tied to the backs of the pedalers. The wee ones arrived in baskets or strapped to the backs of their mothers. Others walked for miles.

And so it was, that morning the white doctor from across the way awoke to the realization that the gap between himself and the people to whom he had come to minister was fast being bridged.

So, ready or not, here we come! The medical work was launched in Lobi Land.

18

The God of peace was always with him,
Even then that bright sun morning.
"Here's my sick," they boldly told him.
And he took them--just that simple.
From that morning, on to sundown,
From that day, on to the next one.
One week led thus to another.
        The days pass so among the Lobis.

–2–

The Doctor
In Lobi Land

Dan Merkh, missionary builder who had arrived with his family several months earlier to build the house and dispensary, cautioned the doctor about beginning his medical practice in Lobi Land. "I don't know how you will get your patients," he wrote to the young doctor in France who was finishing up his language study. "It isn't likely they'll beat a path to your door."

Dan observed the scene that morning and frankly admitted his previous statement had been in error. The yard filled with people crying for attention, and the doctor's first thought was, "But this isn't how I planned it."

By no stretch of the imagination could the doctor be called impulsive. Not only does he take great pains with everything he does, he has been known to give them as well. Perhaps that's why his wife never encouraged his help in the kitchen. If he didn't ask in so many words, his manner implied, "How can you be sure that's the right amount if you just toss it in like that?"

Or, "Did the recipe say to do it *that* way?"

Or, "Is it really ready to pan out? Has it risen *twice*?"

Of course, dish drying fell into a different category!

The doctor's experience in the operating room carried over into the kitchen. He approaches a recipe with all the seriousness of a major operation. Once he made a cake--a cookbook illustration creation with white layers filled with divinity, topped with fudge frosting and flecked with pecans. Ere he lifted the spoon for that initial beat, he had read every comma in the recipe (he almost knew the thing by heart), arranged the equipment in

20

the order prescribed, checked and re-checked the measured ingredients, and driven his wife to the bedroom with an absorbing book.

In like manner, he had formulated a recipe to follow in their new venture in Lobi Land. It went something like this:

Get family fairly comfortably settled in a home.

Finish teaching the children their Calvert course, enabling them to enter boarding school in the fall—Lynn into the ninth grade, Lynette to the seventh grade, and Larry to the third.

Learn the Lobi language.

Prepare staff and clinic workers.

Equip clinic and stock with necessary medications.

According to his estimated calculations, this should consume approximately one year. Yes, that should about do it. He began to study his recipe and get his ingredients in order. Suddenly, without warning, conditions changed.

Two weeks after his arrival in the country, the sick lay dying in his yard. He had no medical equipment and absolutely no medicines, not even a personal aspirin. The family camped in makeshift quarters, and the children's textbooks were still packed away in a barrel somewhere. It seemed he was raising the spoon to take the initial beat with neither his paraphernalia nor measured ingredients at hand.

Yes, doctor, the most closely followed recipe sometimes calls for modifications—the syrup threads before the egg whites are whipped; the fudge hardens in the pan; the eggs do not separate properly. What do you do? Certainly you don't dump it all. You make the best of it!

He knew very little history of these people surrounding him. Before colonial governments vied for boundaries, the Lobi tribe occupied the vast area of land in the savannah area of Western Africa that is now known as Ghana. The Lobi tribe, a faction born of the Tense and Koulango tribes, left Ghana to dwell on the other side of the Volta River. They migrated southwest until at present they occupy the western border between Upper Volta and Ivory Coast. Their number had been estimated around 200,000 people. The thought of 20,000 of these being the sole responsibility of his mission staggered him.

He raised his eyes and surveyed the eleven acres of land the village chiefs had donated to the mission. A mass of scrawny trees, thick underbrush, and termite mounds stretched before him, except the clearing for his house, and over there about 100 yards where the clinic was being built. He envisioned—someday he knew it would be so—landscaped property, neatly cut grass, gardens of flowers. Other homes would be added, as well as quarters for workers and patients' families. His dreams reached for the sky and included a well-staffed, fully equipped hospital to shelter these sick ones now prostrated before him on their dirty mats.

All this, of course, he saw in a glance. He did not notice his thumb was nervously rubbing the ends of his fingers, searching for a rough edge to chew. His mind seems conditioned to this reflex. The second he starts chewing, the machinery of his mind shifts into gear. If you want to know how active his brain has been, examine his fingernails.

"Caw Caw!" came the greeting accompanied by the quick slaps of the hands. The patients were demanding attention.

It was well that a long time ago Christ became an indwelling presence and not someone he met beside his bed or around the table at devotions. In this crucial moment, he recognized this Presence as a source of strength and guidance and confidently took his first step toward the door.

Dabolo sat in the dust holding his daughter's unconscious body. The tense anxious look in his eye as he extended the limp child brought a lump to the doctor's throat. This then was the fellowship of suffering of which Dr. Schweitzer sometimes spoke. He who has experienced relief from pain and suffering is now being called upon to help others experience a like measure of relief. He had spent years learning how. As he met the entreating eyes of the father and touched the dark, feverish body, a prayer rose from his heart. "Oh, God, may the love of Christ be translated into a tangible, visible thing that they will desire and personally claim for their very own."

"What hurts her?" the doctor asked.

A blank stare.

Immediately he met head-on with his first obstacle—the

minor detail of communication. For thirteen months he had studied French only to find that only the educated spoke this language.

"Does anyone here speak French?" he asked as he searched the bystanders.

"Un peu, Monsieur," a school boy responded and was drafted as an interpreter.

Perhaps it was well that day he didn't know the complications of the tribal situations. Perhaps once clear distinctions separated tribe and language, but centuries of intermarriage helplessly confused the race and language until it is doubtful if one can fully determine a pure blood. It's not surprising to find eight different tribes speaking eight different languages in an eight-mile radius.

For convenience these tribes are subdivided into culture brackets, thus connecting the Lobi tribe with the Lobi-Loron or the Lobi-Koulango with some Tenses and Birifors thrown in. To further add to the confusion, you will find groups of villages with the Lobi culture speaking the Loron language or the Loron culture speaking only Koulango. Someone complicated God's plan after they left off building the tower of Babel.

The government nurse stationed in Doropo rose to help in this hour of crisis. This man was charged with the responsibility of helping eradicate three of Ivory Coast's curses—sleeping sickness, smallpox, and leprosy. Because the nearest medical facility was 150 miles away, he also dispensed a few other medicines. He willingly offered the doctor his meager stock which included a good supply of sulfa tablets, a choice drug in the treatment of this type of meningitis. These, coupled with prayer and a good measure of TLC, tender loving care, he showered upon the sick. What he lacked in medication, he made up for in attention.

One evening a few weeks later he lingered as his last patient disappeared down the road. He watched the sun set and felt warmly at peace. The crisis had passed. Yes, he had just dispensed the last of his medicines, but no new cases had been reported for the past two days. The others were well on the road to recovery. In the name of Christ he had willed them to live, and to his knowledge, there hadn't been a single death among them.

He radiated excitement at the possibilities this new work offered.

Little did he know that the real crisis was yet to be faced.

That same night, our son Lynn, 13, awakened us by calling, "Daddy . . . Daddy."

The doctor trembled as he made the examination—sore throat, stiff neck, and spiking a 104° fever. The classic symptoms of spinal meningitis!

A crisp chill hung on the air and dampness lay at his feet as he trudged to the clinic in that wee morning hour. Setting the smoky Aladdin lamp on a neighboring barrel, he rummaged through our unpacked baggage for the microscope and lab set which would aid in confirming the suspected diagnosis. Questions whirled in his mind—had he been able to save others only to lose his own son? If Lynn were in the States, what would he have? A sterile hospital room, choice medications, laboratory facilities, emergency equipment, and yes, consultation with specialists. Never had he felt so deprived. Was this akin to the loneliness of the Savior as He hung on the cross and cried, "My God, my God, why have You forsaken Me?"

No, he hadn't been abandoned. The full moon illuminated the winding path as he retraced his steps home. This illumination seemed to symbolize the overshadowing presence of the Holy Spirit who promises, "I will never leave you nor forsake you." And again, "Lo, I am with you always." That's *now*! This experience alone with God in the moonlight solidified God's will for his life. Even in the midst of this crisis, His peace washed over him with an overpowering force.

The next morning Dan Merkh volunteered to make the long, dusty trip south for medicines. By pushing himself and the car, he turned in our driveway just after nightfall. Prompt medications blended with plenty of prayer resulted in Lynn recovering without even an unpleasant memory. When he asked for a book to read and his favorite dessert—blackberry jello with Dream Whip—we knew the crisis had passed.

After a few months the Merkhs' first furlough came due and they left for America. The responsibility of the unfinished house and clinic, the well and the fence fell into the doctor's lap.

So much to do and so few to do it. The pace appparently

was set for life on the Doropo station, for it diminished little with the years. There was never a time when one could slap one's hands together with a "That's that!" The work never ended.

Somewhere he learned there is virtue in self-dependence and if you want something done well, do it yourself. It would take more years than this first one before he could comfortably delegate responsibility. I wished many times he could lay off responsibility as easily as he laid aside his wrist watch upon retiring. Responsibility lay about him as a heavy cape with an awareness he could not shed. Sleep came easily the minute his head touched the pillow, yet often in the middle of the night, he'd awaken, and conscious of the heavy cape, pause to ponder his problems.

How does one dig a posthole through laterite? What's the best method of digging a well? How do you teach an experienced carpenter that you don't scoop out a door when you have a bowing door jamb? And that little boy with the oozing facial ulcer—has it reached the bone? What's the best treatment? After deliberating on these for a time and consulting with the only Specialist available, he'd slip back into sleep. It was as though he could face anything as long as he was prepared for it.

Of necessity, the missionary must be a jack-of-all-trades. His advice to missionary candidates is: "Learn as much as you can about as many things as you can for at one time or another, you will need it on the mission field."

Although only formally trained in theology and medicine, he became better-than-an-expert in many fields. He's my choice of carpenter because the finished product is sturdy and according to the design; of an electrician because the work is extremely safe and the switches are straight; of a plumber because it looks nice as well as being practical; of a mechanic because he not only knows what he's doing but why it's done that way; of a packer because he squeezes the most in the smallest space, yet arrives in excellent condition; of a layer of tile because he follows a line and utilizes the scraps; of a painter because he cleans up his mess.

He never became an expert clock repairman. Once he tried to take apart a clock which had become extremely noisy about its

25

business. When the last morsel of metal had been re-inserted, it was ominously silent . . . and ridiculously inaccurate. Matter of fact, it eventually threw up its hands in total resignation and made no further pretense. I decided at that point, I would trust him with my body, to cut, probe, and repair at will, but please leave our clocks alone.

He's the first to recognize his limitations and rarely tackles a job he can't handle. He's not apt to attempt welding without a little more know-how. Masonry is not his line. And he's not likely to take another clock apart.

Someone asked him once, "You're a surgeon, aren't you?" to which he replied, "Let's just say I do surgery."

The sick received the lion's share of his time. Construction ceased while he sutured an arm, the fence building halted while he delivered a baby, school teaching postponed while he treated a snake bite victim. The children delighted in these interruptions, especially Larry who would disappear into the uncleared land with his BB gun or butterfly net. Tarzan of the jungle had nothing on him!

All these experiences so early in the doctor's medical missionary ministry made him acutely aware of his dependence upon Divine aid. The utter lack of all to which he had been accustomed was magnified by his limitations. That people got well at all was a miracle in itself. Daily experiences reminded him that the doctor may diagnose, prescribe treatment, and dispense medicines, but in the final analysis, it's God who does the healing.

Thus without planning or preparation and hardly an awareness of it, he launched his ministry in this remote corner of Ivory Coast among one of her most primitive tribes. This wasn't the glorified life of a missionary. Life was stripped clean of adventure and glamor. Everywhere he looked, he witnessed filth, squalor, superstition, and paganism in the raw.

And yet he wouldn't have traded places with anyone.

PART II
A MISSIONARY IN
THE MAKING

It was here the seed was quickened.
In rich soil it thrived and blossomed.
Struggled hard against temptation,
Won the battle for deliverance.
What was done was only planned for,
By a Power strong within him,
T'was a shaping and a grooming
    For his life among the Lobis.

-3-

Roots

Kirksville, Missouri 1928-1946

Lobi Land, West Africa, loomed a world away from Kirksville, Missouri, where the doctor had his beginning some 34 years before. His roots lie buried deep in the rolling hills of Adair county where, at the turn of the century, immmigrants from Czechoslovakia, England, Ireland, and Germany united in double matrimony.

"With blood from all those nationalities running through my veins, what does that make me?" he used to ask.

John Miley, the great-grandfather, was born on a freighter crossing the Atlantic from Germany in the year 1837. German immigrants tended to move in groups and settle in colonies. Settling first in Lancaster, Pennsylvania, and later joining a group headed by Rev. William Kell, the Miley family helped form a communistic colony in Shelby county, Missouri. When this commune mushroomed out of comfortable proportions, 25 volunteers followed Dr. Kell to Adair county to form the historic Nineveh colony. The Mileys composed part of this group.

Nineveh sprawled along the banks of the Chariton River which provided steam power, the largest single source of income. Industries included weaving, tanning (both a glove and shoe factory), and coal mining, although mines were only tapped for the colony's needs.

This elaborate colony, comprising more than 2,000 acres, was designed with a central square from which radiated eight streets. In order to protect their German heritage, language, and traditions, they established schools, flew their own flag, and abided by their own laws.

John Miley grew to manhood in this environment. However, his romantic interests turned outside the colony to the daughter of an Irish immigrant. Mary Snyder, born in Pennsylvania, moved to Adair county at the age of six. After their marriage, he opened a flour mill. During the Civil War he was exempt from duty since he solely operated the mill. Three daughters and a son were born to this union.

About this time, 28 years after its establishment, Nineveh colony showed signs of decay. Discontent with their despotic leader spread to every corner of the colony. A massive smallpox epidemic actually struck the death blow. When Kell's two daughters died, he deserted to the West Coast, thus dissolving the country's most unique colony. However, even after almost 100 years, its physical trace is most apparent in the community.

The only son of the flour mill operator, John, LaVerne's grandfather, farmed for some time and then turned to the coal mining trade. A man of comparative wealth, he established his English-born wife and five children in a 20 room mansion just a stone's throw from the original Nineveh.

John Evancho, just barely 17, sought passage on a trans-oceanic freighter from his native Czechoslovakia. Perhaps when he bade his family good-bye he knew he would never see them again. He strongly believed in America as a land of opportunity, and this conviction was enough to merit braving the dangers of sea travel and the nightmare of entangling all that red tape on Ellis Island. Alone, frightened, confused, he barely understood when the customs official chopped the "cho" from his name. His first taste of personal Americanization.

Heading westward, he migrated to the coal mines of Iowa. A mining accident forced him to the farmlands of Northeast Missouri. Here he met a prim lady of Irish descent who filled the aching void in his life for someone to call his own. Their eight children also helped considerably.

The second of these, Lena, left school at an early age to become a domestic in the Miley household. In a fairy tale romance, the second-to-the-oldest son of a rich man met the second-to-the oldest daughter of a poor man and they fell in love. Following marriage, they set up housekeeping in a tiny two-room house which was their home for more than 50 years. The original structure is unrecognizable, for many changes occurred through the years. With each child born (two) a room was added, then another, a porch, a pantry, another porch to be enclosed, and finally, a bathroom which never completely replaced a reasonable substitute for the one outside.

Herman, LaVerne's father, inherited some of the German concern for minuteness and detail. Being endowed with a shrewd business head, he showed little interest in either farming or mining and opened a general merchandise store instead. Taking neither vacation or days-off, he operated this store up to the day of his death at the age of 70. He was noted far and wide for his honesty, clean living, sense of humor, and gift of gab. A toot of the horn would send him fairly skipping to the store. Black hair parted down the middle, perpetual smile, and always wearing (except on Sunday) old-fashioned gallused overalls and high-top shoes trademarked him. Old-timers, as well as the young, came from miles around just to sit and talk a spell.

In appearance the store changed very little over the years. The overhead billboard extending the width of the store reads: Herman Miley, Fegley, Missouri, reminiscent of the days when this area boasted a Post Office. Inside you walk on the original oiled wooden planks. Other nostalgic evidences are gone. The wooden vinegar barrel, the sorghum buckets where prospective customers sampled the contents with match sticks, the candy case and cookie boxes, the cream tester, cast iron flat irons and other antiquated stock have felt the obliterating traces of time.

The potbelly stove monopolized the rectangular room. A generous sprinkling of straight back chairs frankly encouraged loitering. When the partnership dissolved in death, his mother encouraged the neighbors to linger over cold drinks, candy bars, and ice cream. Even that has been discontinued.

Small, wiry, and energetic with tight accordion pleated hair (which she bestowed upon her son), his mother is a good cook and excellent housekeeper. Also a born worry wart. She was a devoted wife. As a mother, she has been completely unselfish in her love and protection of her family. She chooses the neck (or head, as she also serves this delicacy) of the chicken and makes

31

you feel she honestly prefers it in order that her family might enjoy the choice pieces. Frugality is inbred in her nature, and she saves everything from twine to electricity. Her world revolves around her home, family, church, and, until she closed the store five years after her husband's death, the store. Today she lives in a senior citizens housing complex a few miles from where she began life.

LaVerne's academic life began at the age of four. His older sister by three years took her little brother by the hand and walked him a mile down the road to the little country school. The first year he completed Primer (runner-up of kindergarten) as well as first grade. His second year, a sympathetic teacher boosted him ahead by several notches. In a one room situation, classes took turns reciting. Ambitious students, if they chose, could keep up with other classes as well. The five year old recited with and finished three grades that year. Next fall, at age 6, both he and Mildred entered the fifth grade. His schedule continued at a normal pace after this spurt.

Although scoring over 130 on his IQ test, he carried his knowledge like a credit card—in a private compartment and only displaying it when necessary. Since he was large for his age and completely innocent in his intelligence, he was accepted for what he was—a normal boy who chased fireflies on a summer evening, liked wrestling, dare-base, and ice cream when his family made their regular Saturday night supply trip into the town ten miles away.

His memories of grade school are pleasant and nostalgic. Not so of his junior and senior high school days. You can take a boy out of the country, but you can't take the country out of the boy. Each class in a different room taught by a different teacher took some getting used to. The long bus ride to and from school allowed time for study which he did a lot of in those days, as well as flirting with that slim brunette who never shared his seat but who was always within eye range. This silent courtship discouraged teasing, but Mary Esther was his girl for several years and though they exchanged many gifts, they never once had a formal date.

Upon graduation from high school at age 14, he ranked third

in a class of 124. Honors included the Bausch and Lomb honorary science award and a scholarship to Northeast Missouri State Teacher's College (later changed to Northeast Missouri State University).

He met the first cross roads of his life at the age of 10. During the annual revival meeting at the Hazel Creek Union Church with Winford Davis as evangelist, he realized that God was entitled to his heart and life. Here he knelt at an old-fashioned altar of prayer and became a new creation in Christ Jesus. This made a deep impression on his parents who had become lackadaisical in their spiritual life. Sunday gradually came to be the busiest day at the store with God shoved into a corner.

The new convert took this new way of life seriously and consistently put into practice each Christian principle as was revealed to him. Not long afterward, the rest of his family accompanied him to church and experienced genuine conversion. When he joined the church, his parents put behind them a Presbyterian heritage and joined him and his sister. It was a turning point in their lives. The doors of the store closed thereafter on Sunday, never again to be a thriving day of business.

By the time LaVerne enrolled in college, his interests had definitely swung to the sciences. His practice teaching assignments included a calculus class as well as math which he taught in college that summer.

His extra-curricular activities were few. He joined a stamp club and began a stamp collection which in later years developed into a family project (with Mama doing all the work). Sports mildly interested him, and he made the second team in basketball.

The word *clean* hung over him like a halo—clean in body as well as habits. He was no Holy Joe, yet never felt it necessary to smoke, drink, curse, tell off-color jokes, or indulge in sex to prove anything. He never judged the rightness of a thing because of its popularity. His firm convictions were never imposed on others.

He was pledged to an honor fraternity at the beginning of his sophomore year. Personal witnessing was not emphasized in those days, but an inner persuasion convinced him it was the thing to do. This fraternity would be his proving ground, he reasoned. Ignorant of how to go about this business of soul winning, he didn't go at all. Gradually he found himself drawn more and more away from his convictions.

"What happened to my desire to lead my friends to the Lord?" hit him one night as he participated in one of their sponsored dances. "Why, this is no place for a Christian," he concluded, and walked out the door and down the street to his grandfather's house where he often spent week nights.

With no one to guide him but the Holy Spirit, he sought the answer from God's Word. The response, so quick and sure, fairly exploded before his eyes. A verse, hitherto unknown, stood out in bold relief:

Wherefore come out from among them, and be ye separate, saith the Lord, and touch not the unclean thing; and I will receive you (2 Corinthians 6:17).

He had never before or since had the answer given in so forceful a manner. Okay. God had spoken. He would separate himself from this fraternity—And he did.

That following weekend the little country church again assembled for their annual revival meeting. On Friday night, a hunger and thirst to personally experience God's love and forgiveness flooded his being. When the invitation was given, he walked up the aisle and knelt at the familiar altar, but peace eluded him. Driving home and into the night, an intense preoccupation filled him, "God, where are You?"

Whatever activities he did next day were done half-heartedly because this nagging thought gnawed at him, "God, where are You?"

He was alone in the house. The rest of the family was at the store. God chose that moment to manifest Himself to him as a feeling of warmth and peace invaded his being. He had sought Him and found Him. Never again would he doubt. Years later the experience was still so precious that even the remembrance of it would almost bring tears to his eyes.

The call of God was very real in his life and one he has never questioned. It came during the end of his first year at college with the strains of a stirring revival meeting still heard in the air. One night he was awakened by someone calling his name. His sister occupied the bedroom, and he slept on a daybed in the dining room. He listened to the silent night, afraid to stay awake and afraid to go back to sleep. He was arrested by the certainty that God wanted him to preach. Was this how Samuel felt those many years before when God spoke to him in the darkness? He searched back through all his kinfolk. To his knowledge, no one on either his mother's or father's side had ever entered the ministry.

He didn't intend to be the first.

That decision being made, he tried to evade the call of God. The following year was the most miserable of his entire life. He interpreted God's intervening in his life as interfering. Confusion and bewilderment colored his days. Since he found peace nowhere else, he decided to talk to his father about this, who, in turn, called in the pastor of the church. This dear man really messed things up by announcing that LaVerne would preach his first sermon at the church that very next Sunday, June 17, 1945. Pastor Dobbs had observed the struggle in the young heart and knew that only in the practice of the call could he find the release he sought.

The young preacher recalls that the night threatened rain. He almost wished it would! The church was located on a dirt road, and all the publicity about Missouri mud is true. Too much rain makes the roads impassable, and the church services are automatically canceled. The rain didn't materialize, however, so he took his text from 1 Corinthians 13 (following outlines provided by the Thompson Chain Reference Bible) and must have talked all of ten minutes!

Opportunities for Christian service were limited. He became active in the only religious organization of that time, The Adair County Council of Churches, and served as secretary of the Young Peoples Council.

The acknowledgement of the call to preach put a damper in his plans that last year of college. Being a math major, he had been invited to accept a teaching position at the Rolla School of Mines and enter the field of engineering.

"I can still preach," he reasoned. He could drive home for weekends and pastor two small churches which were struggling for lack of leadership. He already filled the pulpit in these two. This logic perhaps reflected his desire to maintain close home attachments.

A former student of Free Will Baptist Bible College, Nashville, Tennessee, encouraged him to consider this school. R. B. Crawford, executive secretary of his denomination, visited his home area and likewise strengthened this conviction. There was little to appeal to him. The school offered nothing toward accreditation, and he knew no one there. But most important, it was a long way from home. He had never spent more than one consecutive night from home in all his life and this only three or four times. He would not have wanted to be called a Mama's boy, but he was.

An uncle wanted to take him and his sister to the Des Moines, Iowa State Fair, a grand total of 150 miles. LaVerne refused to go. This uncle commented later, "Who would have thought that LaVerne would have been the one to go the farthest away from home and stay the longest?"

Although no definite plans were made for attending the Nashville college, he did change his minor from science to English. He kept his math major. Years later when in theology and later engaged in a teaching ministry, someone remarked, "Wasn't it a shame you wasted all those years in science?"

Not at all. We only see what is apparent. The Master Weaver sees the completed design. Our lives follow a definite pattern traced by His almighty hand. He knows every punch of the needle with no mistakes to be ripped out. Ten years later when LaVerne entered the field of medicine in preparation for missionary service, he learned he had already completed the requirements for Pre-Med, with the exception of a Biology course and another in Organic Chemistry.

Although not overly ambitious, he studied hard and made excellent grades. Since good marks earned extra credits, he received his Bachelor of Science degree at the end of the summer following his third year. He was not yet 18.

The following August found him heading his car, not toward Rolla after all, but toward Tennessee. It wasn't Africa—yet—but it might as well have been, the way he felt.

36

Years later he gave this testimony:

"I don't suppose that ever a boy loved his family and home more than I. What fond memories I cherish today of those boyhood days. There were just the four of us—my mother and my dad and sister and I. But Christ became real in our home while I was still quite young. Those things that have ruined so many homes today—drinking, carousing, cursing, fighting—these were unknown in our home. Instead I fondly remember love, kindness, encouragement, the family altar—things for which I shall be eternally grateful.

"But the day came when I had to leave home. I was only 18, but the Lord had placed the conviction in my heart that I needed to go away to our Bible college to prepare for His service. And so I went. From that day to this, home has never been quite the same. I've been back for visits, but always to leave again for the place of service that the Lord has appointed. It's not that I love my home any less, it's not that I love my family less than in my boyhood days. It's simply that I love Him more."

Passing Rolla, he chose Nashville,
Turned his back on engineering,
Looked ahead to be a preacher.
These were days of fey beginnings,
Friendships formed to last a lifetime.
      There was one, a girl who loved him.
"Let us walk this path together,"
Thus he offered; she accepted.
This was all just preparation
      For his days among the Lobis.

finish

–4–

The Educational Die Is Cast

Nashville, Tennessee 1946–1947

That September of 1946, his mother and father with John and Mary Filkins and his girlfriend, Olena Filkins (who later married Jim McLain and went to Japan as missionaries) attended the annual State Association in south Missouri. From there they proceeded to Nashville to drop off the young student. This first period away from home produced strong misgivings as he watched the car pull off without him, turn the corner, and disappear in the traffic. A trace of a childhood memory clutched his heart momentarily, then disappeared. The orientation of a new way of life and the activities of his new family swept him up so completely that he honestly says he never once experienced homesickness.

Free Will Baptist Bible College, in its fifth year of history, consisted of two converted residences in the fashionable West End section of town. Although representing radically different backgrounds and areas, the 26 students comprised one big family. Since the strict Bible program only offered an ETTA teaching certificate, the registrar assigned the college graduate to the best they had to offer from their two-year program.

Never before and probably never since has his life been so affected in such a short time. From his limited experience, he had observed Christian work as only a sideline. Here it was a commitment. The real value of his stay is not recorded on his transcript. His life merged with other young people who shared his interests and convictions. Like Elijah, he had experienced the "I, only I" syndrome. Teachers and staff displayed genuine interest and concern. Lifetime friendships were cemented.

Psychologists warn of two critical periods in every life—at the age of 17 and again at 45. In this first period a person is acutely aware of his physical and mental developments, customs become habit and one's character die-cast. A man's character never changes radically from youth to old age. He emerges from a series of situations and afterward acts in a consistent manner. Whatever else LaVerne may accomplish in life, I doubt very seriously he will deviate from the pattern established that first year at Bible College. Three of LaVerne's outstanding characteristics surfaced this year to help make him what he is today.

Dr. J. P. Barrow, a real saint, taught Bible Synthesis. Educated at Moody Bible Institute and strongly influenced by the Holy Life teaching emerging from Keswick, England, Brother Barrow's eyes fairly glistened and his face shone as he tried to lead each student into a deeper knowledge of the Spirit-filled life.

As he presented this bird's-eye picture of the Scriptures, the students were encouraged to read the Bible straight through without pausing for research or back-tracking. This admonition extended to a required eight hour reading weekly (by the clock) with a report given first thing on Monday morning. If ever anything would tempt a person to be dishonest, this was it.

In the first place, LaVerne doesn't particularly enjoy reading. Perhaps once reading was a pleasure. At least he owned a near-complete set of Big Little Books (forerunner of comic books). But somewhere along in Academia, reading became something on which to receive a grade, thus squashing its entertainment appeal. Give him a choice of reading the latest best seller, regardless of how religious, or cleaning the storeroom and he'll take the storeroom every time.

He's a slow reader. He reads everything as if he's to be tested on it. Later during his seminary and medical school days, he knew time allowed for only one reading and that one time had to be thorough enough to excel on examination. He reads mail in this manner. If he hasn't time to read it thoroughly, he waits until he does.

The only course he ever dropped was during his last year at

college. "Contemporary Writings" required reading one novel weekly. That was just too much! Likewise this eight hours of required reading each week almost sent him to the registrar's office, except Bible Synthesis was his most vital course and one he needed the most. Even though the required reading was from God's Word, it didn't diminish the fact that it was part of a required class assignment.

Ingenious (or desperate) students devised all sorts of methods to incorporate their hours. Round Robin reading sessions, one reading as the other engages in another activity, as driving, etc. Evidently he never hit on the ideal method because his reading report most always was deficient. Whether or not some students reported dishonestly was beside the point; this was something between him and his God.

Dishonesty is such a little thing, but it is essentially what caused a great city like New York City to default.

For want of a nail the shoe is lost,
For want of a shoe the horse is lost.
For want of a horse the rider is lost,
For want of a rider the army is lost.

Some wish he weren't such a stickler for honesty. A new clerk or cashier, frustrated with new responsibilities, doesn't appreciate learning she has given too much change, especially if her boss is standing at her shoulder. He checks menu totals, follows the cashier's prices, and forbid him ever to pay a bill without verifying it! It isn't that he thinks someone is out to get him. He wants to be sure the totals are correct.

Once we entered Ivory Coast with a brand new Honda. We deposited our baggage with a customs company to prepare official papers. The clerk was instructed to record the Honda as an import from Japan. Unfortunately the clerk forgot and wrote it came from America. When the papers passed through customs, a sharp-eyed agent caught this false declaration and slapped a huge fine against the company.

The clerk was so frightened of losing his job he pleaded with the missionary to take his defense and state he wrote in ignorance, he believed it *was* imported from America. Then the fine would automatically be cut in half.

It amuses me to think of the audacity of this clerk in making this request. After the lecture he received, I'm certain he hesitated before he attempted another dishonest act.

In Africa, the children loved to help balance the books at the clinic because they liked the feel of all that filthy lucre (literally). Lynn's ambition as a small boy was to be "the man who counts the money in church." They knew how much cash they were to have, and if their count showed an increase, they beamed as if they had produced it themselves. If they were short, that was too bad. But their father showed concern about too much money as too little because they both indicated an inaccurate report.

You want to know how honest he is? He even returns the money given in error in phone booths!

The second crisis arose the second semester when the student body rebelled against the administration. Friends on both sides strongly pressured him to join their group. Whether it was his basic respect for those in authority, his capactiy to see both sides of an issue, or perhaps he isn't a rebel at heart, he chose to remain neutral.

Dr. Bob Pierce, former director of World Vision, told the National Association before we sailed for Africa: "Dr. Miley had better not go to Africa unless he's willing to kiss the black man's boots." He foresaw the times when the doctor would be called upon to treat with honor and respect those definitely inferior, to accept with patience and humility the fact that their voice, not his, is final.

In dealing with government officials, the doctor discovered some of the most competent, intelligent, highly trained officials you'll find anywhere; likewise he encountered quite the contrary. Even when suffering extreme exasperation, he never failed to show them less than the respect due.

One of the situations that concerned him most on returning for furlough was to witness the breakdown in law and order. He sees capital punishment as a deterrent to crime. When people no longer respect those in authority, you may expect a weakening of every fiber in the cultural framework.

He not only taught by example, he often resorted to precept. Larry completed his ninth grade by correspondence, choosing to remain at home with Lynette during her last year on the field. That fall when Lynette returned to America to attend Bible College, Larry opted for boarding school. That semester he developed a touch of rebellion against the school in general and the houseparents in particular. During his Christmas vacation, the question arose of whether or not he should return. Whether to go or stay, the decision was his. BUT if he chose to return to school, it would be with the understanding he would abide by the rules and regulations of the school. It wasn't a matter of agreeing or disagreeing with them; or whether or not we went along with all of them. It was school policy and as such must be respected.

He went and he did.

His first year at Bible College, Lynn encountered a minor difficulty which developed into a major one. He took advantage of his position as snack shop superintendent and lost his job. His father wrote him:

"My first reaction, naturally, was 'How Unfair!' But, Lynn, there is another side to the matter that you must see . . . I hope you don't feel that I'm harsh and lacking in understanding. It's simply that 'the son whom the father loves' must be chastened at times. I want you to learn from this experience; it has been hard, humiliating and costly. Yet you can learn something from it that will make you a better man.

"In the first place, never expect privileges that are not accorded to everyone else; if they are given you, fine, but don't expect them or take them on your own. Secondly, don't be guided by what someone has done and gotten by with . . . Lynn, I know you are hurt by what happened. But rather than look back, learn your lesson, look ahead and assume the attitude of the Apostle Paul, 'Forgetting those things which are behind and reaching forth unto those things which are before.' You will be a better man for having done so."

This chapter on the molding process of the Free Will Baptist Bible College in this young life would not be complete without mentioning his development in another area. People are aware of LaVerne's serious side, but are surprised to learn he can play pranks like anyone else. The Lord knew all the frustrations waiting him on the mission field, so He allowed his sense of humor to be honed to a keen edge this year at college.

The antiquated plumbing in Ennis Hall, his dorm, operated on a one-way track. One person showering could regulate it satisfactorily, but let two try it and it meant robbing the other. A third one spelled disaster.

From his room, LaVerne heard Reford Wilson and Wade Jernigan enter the showers. When they were soaped down, he sneaked in the bath and manipulated the lavatory faucet which robbed the showers. First he turned the hot water, then switched to the cold.

"Hey, you're taking all the water," shouted Wade.

"I am not. You've got it all. Hey, let me have some," Reford shouted back. And accusations flew back and forth.

When they began to suspect a third party, LaVerne sneaked back to his room and locked the door.

Had it ended there, perhaps the administration would never have heard a word of it. But the two boys, when they couldn't get the door open to the offender, opened the door in another way. Aiming a heavy foot locker down the hall and toward the door, it opened pronto, but alas, badly damaged the door frame which had to be reported. And whose fault was it? Of course.

The third character trait that focused that year in Nashville arose in the area of finances. Although his father footed his school bill, he felt responsible for his extra expenses. Heretofore his public work had been limited to the hayfield. As a student, he took a part-time job at the Happy Day Laundry, not so much to have spending money perhaps as to have his weekly laundry taken care of.

His father had instilled in his son a value for thrift and careful spending. He was careful, but not stingy; generous, but not extravagant. About this time he began to keep a close accounting of money received and paid out. At the end of the month, he could almost account for every penny. In this way he could calculate what he could afford to buy. He developed a repulsion for installment buying and almost never bought anything in this manner, except cars, home, and a cemetery lot. Whatever the need, be it furniture, appliance, or clothes, it waits for cash on the line.

44

Take care of the minutes, and the hours will take care of themselves. In like manner, he believed that the dollars would take care of themselves if we give heed to the pennies. He was careful to see that it didn't breed the very anxiety it sought to remove. He gathers up empty bottles when he goes grocery shopping, yet never collects them elsewhere for deposit. He takes advantage of sales and specials but will not spend 75¢ worth of gas to drive across town to utilize that special coupon. He checks weights and prices and chooses the most economical buy, yet does not sacrifice quality for economy.

Nothing concerned him more than his accountability to God. He often said, "One's personal whims, one's personal desires pale into insignificance when paralleled with what God wants one to do." He considered this first in the use of his time, his energies, his talents, and most evident in the way he spent his money.

When the plans for our home in Africa were presented for approval, he reacted with, "But it's too big!" He spent hours altering the plans, cutting a foot here, one there, knocking out a couple of windows. He wasted his time. Space is valuable in the tropics, and the builder explained it wouldn't save $25.00. Why sacrifice vital air for $25.00?

Second to his accountability to God stood his accountability to the mission. They were trusting almost to a fault. They provided generous allowances above the salary, but the monthly accounting for these funds weighed heavily upon him. If one isn't careful, an expense account can turn into a form of legalized cheating. To him it wasn't how much you could get by with charging off, but how little you could charge off to get by.

Buying a mission car proved an ordeal to be lived through, not enjoyed. First he considered his needs, examined the pamphlets, visited the car dealers, scrutinized the available merchandise (inch by inch), sought advice from others, carefully weighed the results, and finally, presented it all to the Lord. Just because one has walked with the Lord a long time does not guarantee decisions will become more infallible or be more easily determined.

He says, "I learned a number of years ago that the material

things of this life are insignificant compared to the things of eternal value. I enjoy living in a beautiful home. I like to drive a good automobile. But these things that God gives to us are to be relinquished willingly at His bidding. After all, we are just strangers and pilgrims here. Our citizenship is in Heaven."

It was well that these aspects of his character were becoming deeply ingrained. He would need all the help he could get as his life prepared to head in a new direction—that of marriage.

At supper that first evening at college, he met a second-year student who immediately fell to his unsuspecting charms. Courtship, under the guise of working the daily crossword puzzle, led to a proposal of marriage. This perhaps surprised him as much as anyone, for he had resolved to be a bachelor. Although he made the suggestion, she kept it alive with her enthusiasm. They married that following August.

Great men taught him, shaped his thinking,
Helped him formulate convictions,
Settle doubts of creed and doctrine
Based upon the Word, the Bible.
Thus his vision slowly lengthened,
Encompassing those about him.
But it stopped behind the pulpit.
It takes time to heed one's calling
Not yet hearing of the Lobis.
He had yet to know the Lobis.

–5–

Honing The Mind

Chicago, Illinois 1947–1948

That one year at FWBBC strengthened the conviction that further training was necessary. It boiled down to a choice between Northern Baptist Seminary or Wheaton College.

A few weeks before the wedding, he drove to Wheaton and Chicago to compare the two schools. Since Northern's expenses were considerably cheaper, he decided in her favor. We didn't qualify for student housing, not being affiliated with the Northern Baptist Convention, but he did locate a bedroom with kitchen privileges in the home of a fellow student. Harry Gray lived with his wife Audrey and their two small children in the Cicero suburb about ten miles from school. An A&P grocery store at the corner of our block immediately hired the prospective student as a produce clerk.

He was not yet 19, but he hadn't proposed marriage until he was willing to assume all the obligations and responsibilities it entailed.

Saturday night, August 30, 1947, in the Harmony Free Will Baptist Church, Benton, Illinois, Rev. William Buster, a former pastor of each of us, pronounced us man and wife. The first three days of our honeymoon we traveled and slept in three different beds. On Sunday, we drove his parents to their Missouri home, the following day we drove to our cubby hole room in Chicago, and the next day, Tuesday, we both enrolled as students at the seminary.

We quickly slipped into a routine of classes in the morning, work in the afternoon, and study at night. Sundays we worshiped at a Bohemian Baptist church where we both taught Sunday School classes.

Our one-year acquaintance had revealed many of his convictions, but I soon became acquainted with one not hitherto known. He believed (and still does) that the woman's place is in the home and not on an outside job. A few doors down from LaVerne's A&P store, a Bohemian bakery caught my eye. Since food preparation, and especially baking, was becoming an adventure, I dreamed of preparing all these tantalizing goodies myself. It never occurred to me that I wouldn't be working, so I entered and applied for a job, which was synonomous with an apprenticeship. My offer accepted, I was to begin work the next afternoon.

The new husband didn't react as enthusiastically as expected. Even bribes of home-baked kolache didn't weaken him. Almost embarrassed, next day I declined the job.

"As long as we can get by, I'd rather you not work. I want you *here* when I come home," he explained. We *got by* that year, through a year of teaching, another year at school, and then those years when he went back to the Bible College. We still *got by* during medical school, internship, and residency. It never became necessary to take an outside job although at times it meant a total lack of luxuries. Shopping often was a realization of how many things you could get along without, a constant shuffling of getting this *or* that, never able to buy this *and* that.

Northern was conservative in theology those days and the spiritual and educational quality of the professors outstanding. Such men as C. W. Koller, P. Stiansen, J. R. Mantey, F. D. Whitesell, H. C. Mason, A. C. Schultz, W. F. Kerr, L. M. Perry, and Warren Young made a contribution to his life for which he is eternally grateful.

This year he came to grips with his doctrinal position of eternal security. Up to this point he had only been exposed to our denominational position which basically is more Arminian than Calvinistic. The president of the seminary, Dr. Koller, loved and revered by all the students, called him into his office one day. In a private conversation, Dr. Koller lovingly and convincingly presented his Calvinistic position. It was something to consider. Yes, he finally concluded, he did believe that he had been accepted in the beloved, was a joint heir with Christ in the family of God, and that he was eternally secure through the power of divine grace. However, he couldn't get away from the fact that the teaching of Scriptures indicated a person could make shipwreck of his faith and be lost. Not through an act of sin but through loss of his faith.

With this foundation of faith firmly settled and rooted, he began to profit from the theological teachings and ideas of his instructors. Biblically conservative in theology, spiritual minded, warm hearted, and devoted to the cause of Christ, Mrs. Groom, his Greek professor, perhaps influenced most his learning.

Not only was he doctrinally established, he spiritually matured and rose to a new plane of spiritual living.

A familiar chorus goes something like this:

When you're up, you're up,
When you're down, you're down.
But when you're only half way up,
You're neither up nor down.

Tragically this symbolized the lives of many Christians: one day on the mountain top with Christ and the next in the valley of despair. LaVerne kept his spiritual life on an even keel. If he had his spiritual highs and lows, he kept them strictly between him and his Lord. He never gauged his spiritual depth upon the amount of time spent in the secret chamber.

More than anyone I have known, he consistently practices the presence of Christ. Christ is not an influence; He is a living force: a Person living not beside him, but within him. He strictly observes regular times of devotions, personally and as a family, but communion is not limited to those times. As he watches an airplane soar by, as he dresses, or when he's driving, his lips often move in silent prayer. Often he is awakened by a need in the night, whether to intercede or commune, and he slips over the edge of the bed to his knees and talks to his Lord about it.

He places Bible reading in the same category as eating food; one is just as much a daily exercise as the other. Immediately following his conversion, he began reading his New Testament and has missed few days since. He chooses to follow the example of his father who completed the reading of the Bible each year by reading three chapters daily and five on Sunday.

He has this "thing" about the position of the Bible in relation to other books. Something in him rebels when he sees the Bible covered by another book or object. Automatically he removes the Bible and places it on top, even if he is a guest in your home.

The Psalmist's admonition of "Evening, and morning, and at noon, will I pray, and cry aloud" struck him as a good rule to follow. He interpreted this to start the day with morning devotions around the breakfast table, usually following some devotional guide as *Daily Bread*. Noon time is his private missionary prayer hour, although sometimes the family joined him. Evening devotions are in the living room with the family or the two of us around the bed before retiring. Through the years he has consistently led in these devotional periods.

This pattern of family devotions congealed on our wedding night and has continued through the years. Some night, when I too was a student or a new mother, I'd be so tired and sleepy that I secretly wished he'd forget it. He didn't though. One night especially, I felt so ashamed.

We had settled down for devotions. He read a passage, then closed the Bible and handed it to me. "Why don't you read something, too?"

I opened to the Psalms, fingered down the page for a shortie and mumbled it. I closed the Bible, raised my eyes, and found him looking at me with a peculiar expression. What's wrong, I wondered.

"Sound familiar?" he asked with a smile.

Can you beat that? One hundred and fifty Psalms in the Bible and I had chosen to read the very one he had already read! And hadn't even recognized it! Oh, but I listened after that.

He approached devotions in the spirit of, "This is what we've been waiting for!" He didn't always end on that enthusiastic note. One night—he kneeling on one side of the bed and I on the other—he, as usual, was concluding the prayer. Suddenly he stopped. Was he thinking of something to say? It wasn't an emotional reaction, was it? Mentally I retraced his words. No. Then what? When the silence extended beyond a long pause, I cautiously peeped at his kneeling figure, a sleeping figure whose head lay sprawled on the bed between his circled arms. I almost laughed.

Suddenly as if alerted by my amusement, he picked up where he had left off hardly aware of the restful interlude.

This consistent habit, of necessity, brushed off on his family. The children didn't always accept it as meaningful. Sometimes we'd come home late from church, and transferring sleeping children from back seat to individual beds was quite an ordeal. The pajamas and bathroom bit was done in a semi-conscious state, as were their prayers. Daddy would get them started off on their "Now I lay me down to sleep's" and with a couple of nudgings and promptings they'd make it through the "Amen's."

Perhaps the most lasting influence of this first year at Northern came during a service sponsored by the Pacific Garden Mission. The inestimable value of personal witnessing was dramatically visualized, and we were challenged to speak daily to at least one person, if only to hand out a tract. For him, it became a life commitment. Many times he has left the house before retiring because he had not yet spoken to someone that day. Service station attendants, clerks, motel managers, taxi drivers, delivery boys, anyone whose life touches his, will almost always receive a tract and personal witness.

He vividly remembers attending a religous service preceding an execution at the Tennessee State Penitentiary during his Bible College days. A young father of two, a former taxi driver, received the death penalty for murder. In prison he heard the Word of God for the first time and accepted Christ as his Savior. His statement: "I was a taxi driver in Murfreesboro, Tennessee, for so many years and not once did someone talk to me of the Lord" pierced right to the student's heart. That night he vowed, "May no one who crosses my path go to Hell because I failed to witness of my Lord."

He has used basically the same tract entitled, "The Three R's of Salvation," all these years, one that he prepared while in charge of the Practical Work Department at FWBBC. In Africa, he used the French translation.

Once the Lord burdened him for a sick old man who lived

alone in a house near his parents. An alleged atheist, he never once attended church although living under its shadow all his life. The day LaVerne planned his visit, the bottom seemed to fall from the sky, and rains made the roads impassable. So confident was he of the Lord's leading, he laced up high-top boots and trudged across the soggy fields. he was warmly received and found a lonely old man ready to receive Christ as his personal Savior. We received word he died a few days later.

Although many have been brought to the place of decision during his ministry, his gift seems to be more in teaching than evangelism. He especially enjoys counseling. He has no plans for a private practice in the States, but should he do so he feels Christian psychiatry offers a tremendous opportunity to help a vast number of people spiritually.

Acquaintances were made this year at Northern, but no deep-lasting friendships, which is not surprising, since it was a nine-month long honeymoon. Before the year ended we were expecting our first child, so graduation plans were postponed in order for the young father-to-be to seriously take on this new responsibility. Or at least be able to finance it.

"Isn't it sad that LaVerne has dropped out of school?" a former teacher commented. "We had such high hopes for him."

Hope on, we could have told him. The Lord had things to teach him not found in a classroom.

Left the classroom as a student,
To become a grade school teacher.
Though the place was temporary,
It was vital to God's schedule.
Lessons aren't all learned from textbooks,
Often those the best remembered
Are those taught us from experience.
Often came a thought perplexing:
"Is this all that God has for me?"
(The Lobis still a tribe unheard of.)

-6-

Teacher, Preacher, And The A & P

Kirksville, Missouri 1948–1949

If it were possible to relive one year of our lives, this year of 1948 would be the last choice. In his long-term view of life, he was aware that this was a temporary situation, yet he sought to make the best of it.

Mentally, physically, and spiritually, he formulated a well-rounded program. Socially we felt deprived. To keep up mentally, he stepped into the classroom as a teacher instead of a student. He taught all grades at Mulberry school, a rural school in his home district. In addition, he worked part-time as a clerk at the A&P store in town which kept him in good physical condition. To round out his program spiritually, he pastored (or rather, preached at) three small rural churches. To the faithful at Jewel, Graysville, and Sublette: Blessings on you! You were very patient with your young pastor and his immature wife. Thanks for not demanding too much of us.

Our living situation had much to be desired. A Christian business man in the furniture store business and closely associated with our denomination renovated an old residence into small apartments. On his recommendation and sight unseen, we reserved a two-room furnished apartment. No refrigerator, hanging naked bulbs, and if I close my eyes, I can still smell the fumes that arose from that old kerosene cooking stove.

The other room was furnished as a bedroom with nothing, not even a comfortable chair, to suggest it doubled as a living room. Be that as it may, one day it served as chapel as the young preacher performed his first wedding ceremony.

Might as well get things off on a right foot, I decided. As soon as the guests left, I left an open textbook out for the minister to see. It was turned to the section stating that all wedding fees were to be turned over to the minister's wife. The hint was graciously accepted, but apologetically, he confessed that a fee hadn't been given.

LaVerne was extremely devoted to his grandfather Miley and spent much time with him during his college days. His grandfather possessed a great faith, and LaVerne loved to hear him relate his experiences with the Lord. But death had separated him from his companion, and he was alone, well along in years, in failing health, and more than a little homesick for Heaven.

God called him home that year we lived in Kirksville, and the family asked LaVerne to preach his funeral. It was a traumatic experience—not only the fact that the family who had never produced a preacher was now going to hear the first one on such an emotional occasion, but his first son also chose that inopportune moment to make his appearance. Fortunately he allowed a two-hour leeway between the two events which enabled him to dismiss us from his mind in order to concentrate more freely on his beloved grandfather.

A marked Scripture in his grandfather's Bible provided the text for the funeral address:

"Thus saith the LORD, Let not the wise man glory in his wisdom, neither let the mighty man glory in his might, let not the rich man glory in his riches: But let him that glorieth glory in this, that he understandeth and knoweth me, that I am the LORD" (Jeremiah 9:23, 24a).

This verse as much as any other helped mold his character and shape his convictions.

In late spring he wound up the activities of the school year and closed the doors for the summer. This allowed time to become involved in two-week Daily Vacation Bible Schools at two of the churches. We might have been inclined to chalk this

56

year off as barren and unfruitful had it not been for these schools. Converts from here have blossomed forth into full-time Christian service. God honors His Word.

We were aware that this year served as an interlude in his educational career. As summer ended, he found himself becoming more and more enthusiastic about resuming his studies at Northern. One day in late August he drove to Chicago to make all the necessary arrangements. After all, there are more details to be considered when one's status changes from a couple to a family.

The years had taught him many things. Little did he know that this next year would be the most crucial of his entire life.

Then the call came clear and simple.
He responded with assurance.
Came a peace with deep conviction,
"Go ye" meant somewhere out yonder.
Where or how did not concern him,
Where He led him, he would follow.
Though he knew not for a long time,
    "Go ye" meant among the Lobis.

11/26/84

–7–

Studying Again And The Good Old A & P

Chicago, Illinois 1949–1950

This second year at Northern found us sharing an apartment with an elderly Christian widow who lived on the third floor of an apartment building just five blocks from the seminary. Mrs. Crane, a sweet/cranky old lady, doted on Fluffy the cat. It wasn't we disliked cats exactly; we just resented sharing the bathroom with one.

This second year was a difficult one in many ways. Financially, we often needed much more than our last penny. Once I gazed wistfully at some plastic drapes in a store window. Wouldn't they brighten up our drab room? The cost of $1.98 was just as impossible then as something $1,000.98 would be today.

Physically, the young student moved in a continual state of exhaustion. After a morning of classes (about a mile round trip) he'd eat a quick lunch and walk another mile to his work at A&P (good old faithful A&P) then back again around 11 that night. Our late model car was parked in a nearby rented garage, physical energy being cheaper than gas.

If this year with Mrs. Crane taught him anything, it was patience. She would give LaVerne her grocery list. He toted them in his arms the whole mile home.

"This isn't the brand I like," she'd begin as she removed items from the sack.

"I wish you'd gotten a smaller size," was her comment on item two.

"You forgot the grape juice" (or some other item), concluded

59

the ordeal as LaVerne stood over her in silent exasperation. "Oh, I must have forgotten to write it down."

She had no other means to get her groceries so he never refused to bring them, but it sure developed his self-restraint.

Some Sundays, we'd drop her off at her church on the way to ours. "I wish you wouldn't go down this street," she'd complain. "Those EL trains above give me the headache."

Opportunities for Christian service were available in the First Free Will Baptist Church of DesPlaines, Illinois, a drive of about 50 miles each Sunday. The pastor and his wife, Charles and Irene Osborne, opened their home to us, fed us, and occasionally he'd slip a bill into LaVerne's coat pocket.

Spiritually, we groped hungrily to know God's perfect will for our lives. Formal training nearly finished, family growing–what would we do next? God revealed Himself to us not long after the school year got underway.

In retrospect, there had been key moments earlier in life to prepare for this momentous one. Very often our Lord unveils a glimpse into the future when an inner voice seems to whisper, "This is for you." Like the time as a boy when LaVerne gave his testimony at church, the preacher remarked, "From such as these come our preachers of tomorrow."

There it was. A sudden insight.

Or the day, while driving along, and suddenly a vision of himself as a medical missionary flashed across his mind.

Or at the State meeting when the missionary challenge was given. He hesitated to give his life but substituted the $10 bill he had tucked into the secret compartment of his billfold.

Or as he listened to Brother Willey, missionary to Cuba, and momentarily was transported to another land among another people.

During medical school and especially later in internship and residency, colleagues looked at him in wonder when they learned of his plans. "To Africa?" they'd echo. "You gotta be kidding." "What do you get out of that?" Their values in life have a dollar and cents sign attached.

Others wondered about this thing told them and frankly asked, "I'm interested to know just why. Why would you give up a lucrative practice in the States to throw away your life in the African bush?" They cannot see beyond the conveniences, privileges, and opportunities of America.

Others have the somewhat twisted conception that missionaries are only the misfits of society. Not finding their niche here in this country, they seek fulfillment in a foreign country. But this doctor hardly fit this classification. Patients sought him, fellow students respected him, and his instructors admired him.

What was it then that prompted him to devote his life into a medical ministry among one of Africa's most primitive tribes? The answer goes back to that last year at Northern.

We were vaguely interested in missions. Our home churches hadn't helped a great deal, although this was before the great missions awakening. We were not members of the William Carey Missionary Society, and to my recollection, did not attend a single meeting. What interest we had stemmed from the missionaries we had met during our Bible School days. Away from this influence, our missionary zeal had become rather ho-hum.

The president of Columbia Bible College came to Northern for a week of chapel missionary emphases. Although I was not a student, LaVerne made arrangements for me to attend one service. Dr. Robert McQuilkin was simple and dynamic, neither emotional nor overly persuasive that day as he challenged us with Christ's parting words: "Go ye into all the world, and preach the gospel to every creature." He very forcefully presented the claims that Christ makes in the lives of each believer. Then looking us squarely in the eyes, he challenged each of us to personally face up to this question: "What does Christ expect me to do about the Great Commission?"

It was almost that simple. God had his heart; He had his life, and now he gave Him his future. It was well he didn't know how complicated the design of his life would be; he probably couldn't have faced it. God never laid out a plan before him for consideration. He only asked that he submit his life fully and completely to His leadership, then step by step, He promised to guide in fulfilling this perfect plan.

If only all great decisions could be reached as easily as this one. The Scriptures clearly spoke on the matter. Praying personalized it and brought assurance. The Holy Spirit clinched the two to place a firm conviction in our hearts that while others were to stay, we were to go.

We made no public commitment, not even to each other. It was as though we had to become accustomed to this new thing growing within, coloring our thoughts and shaping our future, before we could talk of it.

One night following our devotions, a sacred atmosphere shadowed the bed. The air seemed hushed with expectancy as he lay on his half of the bed and I on mine. Then he broke the silence. "Have you ever thought about *our* being missionaries?" he asked cautiously.

Perhaps there are women who resent the fact that their husbands became preachers after marriage. "He married me under false pretenses," one objected strenuously. Perhaps some husbands find it difficult to acknowledge another call of God after marriage, especially if it means a radical change of plans for the wife. I do know my husband was very hesitant to speak of this thing which had possessed us both for months.

Separately, we had faced and answered the challenge of missions, yet it was virtually meaningless until we dedicated ourselves together to the task. The Lord takes a man and woman and joins them in one flesh. It isn't likely He'll call one to a task as important as this and not call the other. From that day to this, a conviction that this is what God expected of us has been constant and abiding. We could never have stayed on the mission field without it.

About this time the Lord used another missionary speaker to definitely channel the missionary call. That spring we attended our Bible Conference in Nashville, Tennessee. Here Miss Laura Belle Barnard, missionary to India, told how a faithful Bible woman died because there was no medical help available. LaVerne accepted the challenge of reaching people to Christ by ministering to their physical needs. Since Miss Barnard spoke of the urgent need in India, he felt compelled toward this field.

Toward the end of that year he received an invitation from the Free Will Baptist Bible College. They were expanding their curriculum to offer a BA degree in Bible, and the graduate in

Greek was invited to come as professor of that subject.

The personal temptation overwhelmed us. I hoped my enthusiasm wouldn't be termed persuasion. Everything we possessed could easily (with the expert manipulation of the driver) be packed in the confines of the car. With one child and another due shortly, we yearned to put down roots and draw a regular income.

To accept or not to accept? Would it be compromising his call and heading the car, as it were, for Rolla?

No, in great confidence, he wrote his acceptance. We were still young, he reasoned. He considered this just one phase of our preparation, only another flagstone along the winding path to the mission field.

Although he had completed his thesis for the BD degree (*History of Free Will Baptists up to the Merger of 1910*), he still lacked some hours in theology and Baptist History. Arrangements were made to complete these by correspondence. Little did he realize that some 25 years would elapse before these requirements would actually be completed and the degree granted!

We packed our belongings for his new assignment, making a brief stopover in Kirksville to welcome Lynette into our family. We arrived in Nashville in time to celebrate our third wedding anniversary.

The mission field was e'er before him,
And he moved in expectation,
Eager with anticipation.
  But alas, the path was darkened,
And he found himself in stalemate.
If you'd listen, you could hear him,
Hear him crying to his Father,
And his Father, always listening,
Heard the heart cry, and He answered,
  And reserved for Him their third child.
  "This was not the thing we'd prayed for,"
"Did You do this just to show me?"
Now he knew, there was no doubting,
  He would hasten to the Lobis.

–8–

Alma Mater—
Living By Faith

Nashville, Tennessee 1950–1955

Nostalgia overtook us at every turn. We had returned to the place of the beginning. The student stepped into the role of teacher, and those next five years at the Bible College were some of the happiest of his life.

Our first address was a small three-room apartment just off West End Avenue. The side entrance led to a glassed-in sunporch converted to a living room, a large bedroom, and a cozy eat-in kitchen.

We shared the house with a Christian lady and her husband, a couple about our age. Charlotte was a new convert hungry for Christian fellowship so it was inevitable that we became very close friends. She'd come over and rock baby Lynette, and we'd share with her all our dreams of India.

Her husband, an unbeliever and misunderstanding the fellowship of believers, became very jealous of this relationship. One morning when LaVerne went to the garage he found all four tires deflated. Now he doesn't ordinarily back off from a difficult situation, but this warned of menacing overtones. The very next day he came home with, "There's an apartment on Wyoming Avenue that I'd like you to look at." So we moved again. Apartment number seven coming up.

Other than the fact that Charlotte became a lifetime friend (she even came to Africa to help us on her vacation), another incident is significant about that apartment on Poston Avenue.

Our son Lynn married the summer following his junior year

at FWBBC. We were still on the field. He scoured the area for apartments, but finally chose one, as he described in a letter, "fairly close to school, with a small living room and kitchen and a large bedroom." Since we continued to send mail to the college, his location was anonymous.

The newlyweds spent Thanksgiving vacation with Lynn's grandparents in Northeast Missouri. Ramona caught up on family history by browsing through old photograph albums, Lynn's baby books, etc. Imagine her surprise when she came across a picture of a little three-year-old boy posed on a pony in front of his home—the very apartment in which they now lived.

Unbeknownst, Lynn had chosen the same apartment as had his dad twenty years earlier.

Before the year ended, the new teacher's thrifty nature rebelled against paying out rent when he could be making payments on a home. We again embarked on house hunting and contracted for a modest home in a new subdivision in West Nashville. We had moved eight times in the four years of marriage, and our possessions were still confined to the space of a car. They looked so pitifully inadequate sprinkled over those four tiny rooms.

We could choose—inferior quality furniture on the installment plan or good used furniture cash. He opted for the latter. LaVerne went to his first auction sale and returned with a set of bunk beds complete with springs and mattresses, and also a stove. From the Railroad Salvage he picked up a damaged bedroom suite. Our little home was taking shape.

Lynn not only looks like his father, he's turned like him. Years later when Lynn accepted his first teaching responsibility, Ramona wrote that they were buying a new home. Our next letters crossed in the mail—mine saying that if Lynn were like his father, he would go to an auction; hers telling us that Lynn had semi-furnished their new home from an auction.

One night LaVerne and Cofer's Chapel, our home church, planned a surprise. LaVerne took me somewhere; I don't remember where. But when we returned, the Cofer's Brownies had completed the furnishing of our home. Now we had chairs to sit on, a table on which to set food, and a rocking chair to rock our babies.

Most of his waking hours were spent at the college. He rediscovered the joys of teaching and taught with warm exactness. Remembering the influence for good that one year had in his life, he felt a keen concern for each student. He tried to leave the student a better one for having crossed his path.

Although hired to teach Greek, his other responsibilities included Beginner English, Science, Romans and Galatians, and Parliamentary Law. One year he served as acting dean and registrar. Although younger than many of his students, he earned their respect. He only failed one student, and this was carried through with a deep reluctance. After all, it had been drilled into him, "If the pupil has not learned, the teacher has not taught."

He demanded undivided attention in his classes. One student wrote later in remembering those days: "Dr. Miley gave me a zero in Romans and Galatians class one day because I was writing a letter to my mother."

Twenty years after he left the Bible College, he received a letter from a candidate to the mission field. The wife wrote: "We have submitted your name as one of our references. You possibly do not remember me, but I suspect you do. I was the one who went home during the Christmas vacation with _____ after I sought permission to do so and had been refused. You were the dean at the time and were the one to give out the punishment. We had to write our life history in connection with getting this appointment, and my comment about that episode was: 'I don't remember the punishment, but I shall never forget what he had written on the card he gave me as I left his office. That was Philippians 3:13, 14.' "

After his third year of teaching, the 1953 College *Lumen* was dedicated to him:

We feel there are many who have contributed greatly to the growth and success of Free Will Baptist Bible College. However, there is one who has been outstanding, not only because of his devotion to his work, but because of the inspiration he has been to each of us.

For the quiet testimony of his daily life.

For his leadership in our practical work department.

For his scholarship and thoroughness as a teacher.

For his understanding and friendliness to each student.

We gratefully dedicate this volume of our Lumen to Mr. Miley.

One year he combined his teaching responsibilities with pastoral duties. The student pastor of Bethlehem Church, Ashland City, Tennessee, had completed his schooling and accepted a full-time pastorate in another state. The church appealed to the college for pastoral assistance, and Brother Miley was asked to fill in until a full-time resident pastor could be available. The full week's pastoral duties were compressed into one Sunday. Leaving home early, we'd cross the ferry at Scottsboro and drive along the scenic highway near the Cumberland River.

Bethlehem depended on their pastor. One Sunday he served as pianist, Sunday School superintendent, Men's Bible class teacher, and preacher. It's a pity he didn't think he could sing solos; he might have monopolized the service.

We never lost the vision of medical missions, yet the pillar of cloud which had been so clear before was now obscured. What should we do first? How? When? Where? In many ways, these were the happiest days of his life, yet back in his mind and occasionally probing his consciousness came the realization that this was not his ultimate place of service. After a time, however, he became comfortably settled in a place of active, satisfying Christian service. Perhaps he would never have left had I not become pregnant with our third child.

In anticipating medical school, we realized we had outgrown a rented bedroom with kitchen privileges. Expenses would be enormous and a wife with small children would not be expected to seek outside employment even if her husband would permit it, which I was certain mine wouldn't. (P.S. Increased pressure from the Women's Lib Movement hasn't swayed him one bit.)

How does one determine God's will for his life?

One dear saint had a key which worked for her. She would beseech the Lord with a closed Bible. Then opening it carefully to a divinely guided page, the answer would leap up at her. Once she was faced with a decision to stay or go to another place of service. Naomi's admonition to Ruth, "Sit still, my daughter," was the answer for her. The fact it worked sometimes encouraged her to at least try it all the time. It didn't work for us. What personal divine guidance could be found in the tabernacle dimensions or a lengthy genealogy?

Others regularly "put out the fleece." The application of "If you cause such and such to happen, then I'll know that you want me to do such and such thing." Gideon bargained with God. In our extreme helplessness, perhaps this is the bargain we struck with God: "Do this for us and then we'll know." He did it for us and we knew, but not in the way anticipated.

We never deliberately disobeyed God. We simply did not know what was His will. No magical verses pointed the way. Even our past experiences in determining God's will offered no help. How simple it would be if for just a few minutes, our Lord could take physical form and we could gaze at Him squarely in the eyes and ask, "Lord, should I do this?" His audible reply, "No, my child, do thus and so." Or even, "Yes, and I'll go with you," would give us bold confidence to go forward.

But life isn't that simple. And ours wouldn't be a walk by faith if it were.

He reasoned in his logical manner, (1) medical school is expensive, (2) increased family would mean increased costs, thus (3) we should have no more children at this time. Just like that. Lord, if You want us to go to medical school and on to the mission field, then see that we don't have any more children now. Just as we had committed everything else to Him, we entrusted this to Him and asked Him to take care of it.

Wouldn't the Pill or its equivalent have been more dependable? In retrospect, I know that all these things were closely interwoven. We could no more have omitted Him for this aspect of marriage than we could have shut Him out of our devotions.

Was this too much to ask of God? The God of Sarah, Rachel, Rebekah, and Elisabeth was our God, too. He who could open wombs could close them just as well. As we desperately groped for a tangible sign from the Lord concerning our future, we placed all our trust in this arrangement.

A shiver races up and down my spine even yet. We know now it was foolish, but God sometimes answers foolish prayers, too.

It was exciting just to be alive. He loved his work, we loved each other, and we faced the future with blind expectancy. Sometimes when the children slept and the dishes were washed, when the test papers were returned to the brief case and the next days classes prepared for, he'd venture a glimpse into the future. "Where will we get all that money for medical school?" he'd ask himself as he devoured the brochures. The amounts listed were staggering. It was about all he could do to budget his $220 monthly salary.

Then a visit to the obstetrician confirmed what we had suspected for weeks. An occasion which ordinarily brings indescribable joy blanketed our apartment. The tone of our lives changed as well as the course of our future. God had not called us after all. He wanted us neither to go to medical school nor the mission field. Doubt was a fearsome thing as it wound an ugly tentacle into every area of our living. It wasn't that we objected to having another baby or even that we couldn't afford it. No longer did we know God's will when once we had been so certain. Inwardly we groaned at this collision with unanswered prayer.

We learned it wasn't unanswered prayer at all. It was a matter of terminology. Withholding children and withholding pregnancy were not synonomous with God.

Once a few years later in Memphis we faced a similar experience. LaVerne was winding up medical school and faced internship. For several days a silent cloud hung over our household, and my faith again went through a testing period. How could we have another baby NOW? Again it wasn't that I objected to a large family; it just seemed such an inopportune time.

That time LaVerne came home early enough to babysit while I attended a Woman's Auxiliary meeting at the church. I sat beside him on the couch before leaving and said, "There's something I want to talk to you about when I get home."

Of course he knew. That's the wonder of marriage—a blending of minds as well as of flesh. Suddenly a memory of another expected pregnancy leaped from the shadows. Before he pushed it back, he replied gently, "Be careful how you pray." God in His great love and mercy erased this concern from my mind so it never again became a problem.

But the problem became almost more than we could cope with during those Nashville days because we couldn't reconcile it with the will of God. It didn't lessen the excitement, however, as I was admitted to the hospital for the delivery. There's absolutely nothing, nothing that matches the thrill of imminent delivery. At least for the mother-to-be. The nonchalant father of his third complacently left his wife in competent hands and went to the classroom to administer a routine test. We're told Lynn remained just as casual when his two children were born.

Suddenly there in the delivery room, a wave of suffocation swept over me. The look of the aide, the urgency of the nurse—something was wrong. My anticipation turned to apprehension. Was God going to punish me for not being happy about this baby? "Oh, God, forgive me. I do want her. I do love her. Oh, God, I love You." Mercifully a stab of the hypo blanketed my consciousness.

I fought my way back to reality as the pale-green walls pushed back from me. I fumbled the side bars of the bed, then slowly focused on the doctor bending over me. He patted my hand and his words echoed clearly through the haze, "We lost your little girl." His job ended, he left me alone.

We lost your little girl! God *had* answered. He *had* withheld our child. "Oh, dear God, this isn't what we meant!"

Never before had he signed such a paper, this one authorizing an autopsy on our stillborn daughter. How else would we have learned of the congenital abnormality which the doctor assured us would likely never happen again? From her conception this thing was known and planned of Him. And all this that we might know. Her christening dress of white embroidered batiste, her only gift, became her burial one. I cringed to think of bone of our bone and flesh of our flesh being shoved into the dirt like a scrap of refuse.

"Go ye into all the world . . . . " A pillar of fire brightly gleamed through the darkness. "Lo, we looked up and saw . . .

71

and therein we rejoiced." This then confirmed God's will.

We're keenly aware of His part of the bargain as we drive through the winding lanes of the Woodlawn cemetery. We park the car near Rebekah Gardens and search for the simple bronze marker which reads:

Lydia Miley

December 13, 1953

A Perpetual Reminder of God's Will for Our Lives

Psalm 143:10a

She in her death did something that she in her living could never have done.

He lost no time in making an appointment with the Vanderbilt School of Medicine. The chairman of their committee on admissions was most unsympathetic with the idea of medical missions and dismissed him with discouraging and scornful words. "It's impossible to be effective as *both* a doctor and a minister. Make up your mind which you really want to be, for you can't be both."

Although a bit downcast, he was fully persuaded that even though man had rejected his proposal, its source was God Himself, and he could do nothing but pursue it.

He completed his pre-med requirements at Vanderbilt while continuing his duties at the college. A few months later he made official application to the University of Tennessee Medical School, Memphis, Tennessee, and was accepted for the fall term.

Our second son was born before we left Nashville. This fourth pregnancy was special, one unlike any of the others. We needed this baby to have peace with ourselves. We claimed him as God's gift to us, our child of promise. The still small voice of God spoke consolation to us, "I'm sorry we had to take your little girl, but we're giving you this little boy instead." Larry was a covenant of the peace between us and God.

Before leaving the college, the faculty honored the departing teacher with a dinner party at a local restaurant. Later one of the professors approached him and hesitantly asked, "I don't mean to be inquisitive, but just *how* are you going through medical school?" It was a polite way of asking, "How can you afford it?"

72

The jobless, salaryless, ex-professor remembers he was almost embarrassed to reply, "By faith." Perhaps he was a bit presumptuous to launch into this huge undertaking with only the promises of God to back him up. But he had learned that the riches of Glory were at his disposal through the Lord Jesus Christ, and how could anyone ask for more?

The riches of Glory are sometimes found in earthly bank accounts. A month before school opened, he received a letter from a retired doctor and former missionary living in a small mountain town of Paintsville, Kentucky. A check for $300 fell from the crudely written letter which read, "We have heard you want to go into training as a medical missionary. My wife and I would like to pay all your expenses, books, tuition, etc."

He tucked the check in the secret compartment of his billfold until he could meet the unexpected donors. A native of the Show-Me state, this was something he would have to see for himself. He drove to the small town and was directed to a very ordinary frame house with an old model Ford parked in the drive. Could this be the home of the people who casually handed over thousands of dollars to a stranger?

Dr. and Mrs. William M. Keith had set their priorities with eternity's values in view. Wealthy through inheritance, he invested his money, not in stocks and bonds, but in lives dedicated to the service of God. The business transaction, sealed by contract, provided for all expenses of a medical training with the stipulation that he complete two full terms on the mission field. If he were unable to do so, the money was to be repaid with interest.

This fine couple lived to see their doctor by proxy reach the mission field in Africa before God took them home. Only God knows how many times they were able to reproduce themselves in this manner.

Having now completed five years of the happiest days of his life, he now turned toward Memphis for another five-year cycle.

"You can't do it", but he did it —
*Both a doctor **and** a preacher.*
As a preacher, soothed heart problems,
As a doctor, calmed the aching.
Yet what e'er the ministration
It is God who's the Physician.
*   The more he learned, the more he knew this,*
All through med school, through internship,
Followed by a time in surgery,
Like a sponge, he soaked, absorbing,
To release among the Lobis.

–9–

Preacher, Teacher, Medicine Chief

Memphis, Tennessee 1955–1960

The home of the Cotton Carnival became our home for the next five years. He completed the four-year program in medicine in three years and a quarter, served one year in a rotating internship, and an additional six months in a surgery residency.

As moving day drew near, we decided to drive to Memphis to locate housing, etc. Leaving our three children with a baby sitter, we took off with all the enthusiasm of newlyweds choosing their first apartment.

By evening our zeal had waned, matching the slow descent of the sun over the mid-south horizon. Our search had been fruitless, and he pointed the car homeward. Hesitantly, as if reluctant to admit failure, he pulled the car to the curb. He picked up the well-creased classified section that lay between us and commented on one checked possibility which hadn't been followed through. The smirking sun reminded us that we were five hours from our waiting children and sitter, and this particular house was a cut across town in the opposite direction.

"Let's pray about it," he suggested. Then we cut across town.

It was love at first sight. We deposited our $20 to demonstrate our good intentions to take up a VA loan on the house offered by a Baptist deacon and to return later for the closing. The sun bade her farewell as we hit the Nashville highway, her final wink a signal of victory.

The house miracle began one marvelous provision after

75

another. Indeed those five years in Memphis seemed a perpetual answer to prayer.

Financially, we walked by faith. Though school expenses were provided for, the normal expenses of rent, utilities, clothing, and food popped up with alarming regularity.

A few months earlier, LaVerne had visited the Young Married Couples class in the Highland Park FWB Church, Detroit, Michigan (now the Central FWB Church of Royal Oak, Michigan). Here he bared his heart concerning medical missions. Our first month in Memphis we had their response—they voted to assist in the doctor's preparation by sending $100 monthly. This check came as regular as clockwork our entire stay in Memphis. This provided our living.

Those were lean years. Lynn remembers scraping to even find 25¢ lunch money. Yet we were never hungry. Once I despaired because all the larder offered was pinto beans and corn bread. Now that's fine when you *choose* to have it, but when you have nothing else, it alters the flavor. When the meal was finished that day, one of the children remarked, "Boy, that's the best food we ever had." Such a compliment improved the flavor considerably.

That Christmas we drove our six-year-old Plymouth for a visit with LaVerne's family. The old car balked and refused to return with us. Before he encouraged it too much, LaVerne's uncle, a car salesman, warned him, "You'd better trade off that car—now!" He scouted around and picked out a later model, and they discussed terms. "How much can you afford to pay?" the salesman asked.

One never becomes accustomed to financial embarrassment. A quick look at our financial situation revealed we already trusted the Lord for the extra odds and ends that arose each month. Swallowing his pride, he asked cautiously, "Would $25 be enough?" And $25 it was.

Before the first payment came due, we received a letter from the Young Adults class of Fairmount Park, Virginia. It began, "Our class voted to send you $25 each month . . . ."

Philippians 4:19 came to have a special significance. Our needs were met. Our house and car payment were always paid

76

on time, we never skipped a utility bill or even had to pay the fine for lateness, our clothing was adequate, and we weren't hungry. When we went without things—Lynn was almost out of Cub Scouts before we could afford his uniform—we reasoned they weren't actually needs, only wants, and you can't blame God for lack of wants.

One Saturday it looked like God had confused wants and needs. We were out of soap. We had detergent but no bath soap. Although not a Biblical principle, "Cleanliness is next to godliness" was practiced religiously. But if we had no soap neither money to buy any, how does one reconcile that with Philippians 4:19, "But my God shall supply all your need . . . "?

Early next morning we drove to Pocahontas, Arkansas, where LaVerne filled in as supply pastor.

Mrs. Smith, the youth director, came up to me. "Our young people want you to meet with us in our class tonight."

"Sure," I replied, just glad she hadn't asked me to speak.

That evening the teacher apologized profusely as she indicated the cosmetic shower the young people had brought. "Please don't think that we think you're dirty. No one knew what the other was bringing, but it looks like most everyone brought soap." And soap it was—*Lux, Camay, Sweetheart, Lifebuoy,* you name it and we had it. It took awhile to pull my thoughts together. Why do God's promised provisions often throw us off balance?

To this day we have never lacked for soap.

LaVerne never waited for pediatric training to begin caring for the children. When Lynette was born, he took over two-year old Lynn's complete care at night. When Larry came along three years later, he included Lynette in his nocturnal tending. If they needed drinks, medicine, changes, or consoling, he responded. When Larry reached the age of two, Daddy just included his calls in with the others. They seemed to outgrow a need of me, but never outgrew their need of him.

One night in Africa, Larry was sick and as usual, called "Daddy!" The exhausted doctor had just returned from a sick call and in that moment of dropping off to sleep was dead to the world. I went to Larry and asked, "What's the matter, honey?"

He blinked up at me and growled, "What are you doing here?"

That first year in Memphis, Larry faced a crisis that reached beyond even Daddy's ability to help.

In cleaning oil brushes from a craft project, I left a small glass of turpentine in the bathroom. Independent Larry wanted a drink of water and went to the bathroom to help himself, climbed upon the commode, and found a glass already partially filled. A terrifying gagging and choking brought me to the scene. The smell on his breath told me what he was unable to.

I telephoned a neighbor lady who drove us to the closest doctor. Forcing that fat tube down that little boy's throat seemed almost inhumane, but the doctor seemed pleased with the results.

"The danger from these accidents," the doctor warned, "is pneumonia." So he scribbled a prescription to ward off this possibility.

Clutching an empty billfold to me, I asked how much was the office charge. There was no charge, he told me, since my husband was a medical student. "But start the medicine right away," he warned.

When the neighbor offered to stop off at the drug store for the medicine, I casually mentioned my husband would pick it up, indicating the more urgent need to get Larry home to bed.

Larry couldn't stand to be too far away from family activity, so he was "in bed" on the couch when Daddy came home that evening. His concern surpassed mine when I handed him the prescription because his billfold, like mine, was empty. While I dished up supper, he, from force of habit, changed into more comfortable clothes and shoes. When my call to eat went unheeded, I found him seated on the bed and staring into space. Misery loves company, I supposed, so we sat together in silence. Finally he turned to me and asked, "Do you know anyone we know well enough to borrow money from?"

He must be desperate, I thought, because he isn't the borrowing kind. Except from his father to finish seminary and Brother Barrow for a down payment on a house, I couldn't think of anyone he had ever borrowed from—not bus fare, not for a telephone call, not for lunch, not for anything.

I couldn't and slowly shook my head. He must have, for he began to remove his slippers and tie up his shoes.

Suddenly I remembered! "You know sometime ago we got a check from Ken and Lou. What happened to that?"

Hope switched on like light. We almost bumped into each other getting to the desk, leafed through the letter hold, and yes, there was the envelope! We removed the contents. A letter-size sheet of paper with only these words written: "We thought you might need this," signed Ken and Lou Walker. The check was for only $5.00 (we didn't need more), but it had as much value as $5,000.

He already had on his shoes, so he was on the way to the pharmacy.

Some day I may ask him—he had on his shoes that day to go a-borrowing. Whom did he think he knew well enough to borrow from?

"Father knows best" was the last word in our household. He taught more perhaps by example than by precept, although he injected his words of wisdom whenever the opportunity permitted.

He lived by the Ten Commandments, and "Remember the Sabbath day to keep it holy" was never a controversial commandment. No one ever studied at our house on Sunday. Over half of his life has been spent in the classroom, either as a student or teacher, yet he never found it necessary to clutter up the Lord's Day with these secular interests. School books and assignments were privileges (or burdens) to be laid aside at midnight on Saturday night and not to be picked up again until 24 hours later.

He has never seen the ox so helplessly caught in the ditch to justify Sunday purchasing, with one exception. He frowns on Sunday traveling, but when it's unavoidable, he does stop for meals. This doesn't include stopping for a milk shake or ice cream cone a couple of hours later, even if one has been out of the country for four years where Dairy Queens were unheard of.

Father has a "thing" about television. He has never bought a set, and it isn't likely he ever will. That doesn't mean we haven't had one in our home; one has often been made available to us. Harold Graham, a deacon in our church who repaired TV's on the side, loaned one to us during our sojourn in Memphis.

We went over the dangers of television with the children and helped them select the right programs. Programs which consistently emphasized drinking or voilence were banned. Occasionally a favorite program would picture a scene of drinking, and one of the children would sprint to the picture to cover it lest others be influenced.

It was hard to get around the commercials. They learned which ones to avoid, especially tobacco and liquor, and they'd take turns diving for the sound button and doing a hula before the screen until the offensive picture was over. It was a long time before they realized this wasn't the normal procedure in a Christian home.

On our first furlough, Harold again accommodated our children with TV. With two of them! They stood side by side, one for the sound and the other for the picture!

On one occasion, "The Death of a Salesman" was to be presented live on TV for the first time. It was widely acclaimed, and the children even persuaded their daddy to sit down and watch with them. He was home so rarely those days.

With high excitement they planned for this occasion, even to *Pepsi Colas* and cheesy tid-bits. Lynn arranged the seats just so, and we grouped before the sets with all the aplomb of a broadway production.

It was an idyllic evening until the hero came out with a word of stark profanity. Like a slap across the face, it echoed through the darkened room. I felt the children tighten in tension, and not until they were sure their daddy was going to ignore it did they slowly relax.

We neared the climax. The poor man was losing his job and reputation. What ever was he going to do? We strained to help him find a solution. But we never found it that night, for the hero came out again with that offensive word, and this time their daddy did not ignore it.

He walked to the sound set and turned the knob. "What people say or do outside my home, I cannot control. But I cannot allow that language in my own living room."

We had *Pepsi Colas* and cheesy tid-bits without "The Death

of a Salesman." Oh, well, they preferred games anyway.

Medical school is often a breeding ground of atheism, indifference, and backsliding. If one's feet aren't firmly planted by the time he reaches this stage, it's doubtful he will penetrate to any great depths in his Christian experience.

A quick sterilizing method is to lay an instrument doused in alcohol on a tray and ignite it. The flame licks up all impurities, leaving a germ-free instrument. Tragically, several students began their training on a victorious note only to find their Christian experience and missionary call doused with a coating of atheistic professors, profane and worldly classmates, and rigid schedules. In process of time at the point of crisis, the fire failed to purify and sterilize. It devoured almost everything, leaving nothing but a defeated and broken life.

Thankfully, the roots of this medical student's Christian experience plunged deep. He never got out of touch with God though at times he got by on stored-up energy. He regularly attended his chapter of Christian Medical Society, and schedule permitting, he participated in the noon-day devotions sponsored by the Baptist Student Union.

His schedule forbade acepting a definite Christian service responsibility, but he filled the pulpit occasionally. A splinter from the First Free Will Baptist Church was suffering a sporadic growth. In our five years with them, we worshiped in four different locations. Our hearts nearly burst with pride to come home one furlough and view their spacious building spread out over Cottonwood and Perkins. We were part of that humble beginning.

The wise man in Ecclesiastes admonishes: "There is a time to speak and a time to refrain from speaking." It is not always easy to distinguish between the two. At least LaVerne found it so that last quarter when his class met to plan their social calendar. Two occasions were planned—the weekly luncheon held in various restaurants in the city and the bang-up banquet as the grand finale. The choice and amount of liquor for the banquet were selected without a comment from him. It might as well have been staged on the moon for all his intentions to be present. He was the only absented member.

Luncheons were another matter. He had formed close friendships among his classmates, and he longed to share in this innocent time of camaraderie. When the subject of lunchtime cocktails arose, he applied the wise man's admonition and mustered courage to speak his objections. With the exception of very few, all the students either drank or had no convictions against it, yet they all but one agreed to dispense with the lunchtime imbiberie.

One of the highlights of graduation is the presentation of awards. The coveted Vanderburg award is given the student who has overcome the most obstacles in attaining his goal. A friend confided in us once, "I'm praying Dr. Miley will receive this award," which consisted of a fully equipped doctor's bag.

The Lord said no. But a negative answer is not a sign of rejection. It often means He has something better for us.

The medical student graduated with the highest grade average (91.49) from a class of 49. Neither of us had worked or earned a salary during his entire schooling, yet he walked off that platform completely debt-free. To God be the glory.

Graduation with the privilege of signing M.D. after his name was just the beginning. A preacher does not automatically become a warm, wise pastor when he earns his seminary degree. As he shares his congregation's births, deaths, and marriages does he enter into that which he has been called. Neither does an M.D. make a doctor. It grants him the right to claim the title with the privilege of entering into that which will make him one.

That year of rotating internship at the University Hospital proved a good initiation. He translated his absorbed book learning into decisions concerning flesh and blood cases. His Saturday night emergency room experiences treating ghetto accident victims prepared him well for the ghetto cases awaiting him in Africa.

He tried not to become so involved with his patients medically that he overlooked their spiritual needs. One young husband, an accident victim, especially tugged at his emotions. When he was released, the doctor made a 100 mile round trip to lead him to a personal knowledge of Christ.

As his year of internship at John Gaston neared an end, he

felt it imperative he get additional training in surgery before departure for the field. Our mission board had no medical requirements for their medical personnel—he being the first volunteer—so they trusted his judgment. His internship ended December 31, and preferably, he wanted to begin his surgery residence January 1, and preferably in the area where we were already settled. Considering that (1) in November he had made no applications, and (2) most appointments are made a year in advance, it seemed almost an utter impossibility.

He made application to the Veteran"s Hospital in the city. One morning while talking to the Lord about this decision, he felt strongly impelled to call the hospital. Almost immediately he had the chief of surgery on the line. Due to a cancellation that had occurred only moments before, the young doctor was assured of a place on the staff.

That spring as new shoots pushed forth from the damp earth and the trees budded with renewed life, our spirits likewise burst forth with a new surge of enthusiasm. On June 30, his residency would end, and finally after almost ten years of preparation, the mission field would be a reality. We bustled with plans. "Let's see," we thought. "We'll have to go to language study, probably to France. Since classes start in the fall, we should sail by August in order to get settled. My, we'll have so much to do—dispose of house and furniture, buy new things and pack, say good-bye to family and friends." We were so anxious to get started I bought a pair of sandals perfect for Africa, and wore them out before we even left the States.

Then it happened. A sharp slap across the face could not have pained more than the message delivered by the director of Foreign Missions.

One April afternoon when the air was alive with bursts of spring, Brother Rolla Smith stopped by from the annual meeting of the Foreign Missions Board. I welcomed him in high spirits left over from the gesture of my neighbors. That afternoon they had honored me with a *Tupperware* party, their farewell gift to our family.

I'm not sure he would have been so warmly received had I known the news he bore. LaVerne was at the hospital, so I bore the shock alone. Brother Smith read and explained a resolution passed. The inevitable whereases described our need for housing and transporation, clinic and car and education of our three children; finally be it resolved that "the Mileys raise $10,000 before they leave for the field."

Later this became expected procedure, but up to this time when a missionary had his equipment and passage, he was off. Ten thousand dollars! Where would we get all that money? In typical feminine fashion, I began to cry. Brother Smith sought to comfort me. "Now, Lorene," he spoke gently, "you're just afraid you'll have to give all that *Tupperware* back."

My husband didn't react as emotionally as I, but he moved in silence the next few weeks. Our bubbly conversations of France and Africa and clothes and schools were pushed into some corner of our minds. The mission field which just a few days before was within our grasp was now slipping further and further from reality.

The doctor perked up when job openings were announced. The coal mining towns in West Virginia were begging for doctors, offering $1,000 monthly plus housing and fringe benefits (an enormous amount in those days). Could the Lord be offering this as a means of meeting the need? How long would it take to save $10,000? Although the salary looked tremendous, we had learned by experience that one spends just about what he has. At our present standard of living, there was no doubt this vast sum could be accumulated in a year.

Our eyes and ears were attuned to all quick money opportunities. What about quiz programs? This was the era of the $64,000 Question, and we witnessed people becoming rich in a moment of time. No, that wasn't for us. Even the thought seemed degrading.

Well, what about the Methodists? They were seeking medical personnel for their established mission hospitals, and they had more money than ours. We wouldn't even have to go out begging for it.

In July, we attended our National Association in Fresno, California. The doctor gave a brief testimony stating why we were going to the mission field and announcing that now at last we were ready to leave.

That's exactly what our people were waiting to hear.

A brief itinerate was scheduled to precede the annual missionary conference in October where we would be commissioned. Why, the doctor wouldn't have missed this deputation period for anything. For years he had starved for spiritual fellowship, and he licked it up like a deprived puppy. Without once mentioning our need of money, the account soared. It not only filtered in, it poured in. Three months later the amount needed had almost doubled.

And we didn't even have to join the Methodists!

We had pulled up stakes before, but it was never quite as traumatic as this. When Lynette and Kay separated for the last time (they had been inseparable for almost five years), the two of them blubbering and crying and Kay sobbing, "Lynette, please don't go," we had second thoughts about uprooting our children from security.

That three-bedroom frame home had become a part of us those years, and some part of us wanted to hang onto it as a security blanket. A deacon, sensing our indecision, offered to take over the responsibility of the home for us in our absence, thus assuring us of a place to return to on furlough. The Lord made it clear that the cut from all material possessions was to be final and absolute. This included real estate.

So once again, as in the beginning, our possesions, including three children, were literally confined to the space of the car. There's a certain simplicity in this manner of living.

His parting missionary message to that convention, October, 1960, was taken from Psalm 126:6, "He that goeth forth and weepeth, bearing precious seed, shall doubtless come again with rejoicing, bringing his sheaves with him." He concluded that, "If we have no compassion, we don't need to go."

The following month, he left, going forth bearing his precious seed. The tears, both bitter and sweet, were yet to be shed.

It was Christmas in his homeland
Christmas, too, he left in Paris,
Left his family safe in Paris
Crossed the sea and spanned the mountains
Viewed the desert down below him
Saw vast lands stretched out before him;
    All the while his heart was singing
Soon now soon, I'll meet my people,
Soon now soon I'll meet my Lobis.

–10–

Christmas In Lobi Land

1960

He knew before he opened his eyes that this was to be THE DAY. He shivered—as much from cold as anticipation—as a chill shimmered up his back. A little cover might help, he figured, and pulled the threadbare blanket snug around his chin and ears. Who would have imagined Africa could be so cold? Flopping over to his side and adjusting his weight in the nest of the sagging mattress, he mentally prepared for this second day of his trek in the African bush. He had barely arrived in France for his language study preparation before he left his wife and three children to make this quest in search of a site for the proposed medical station.

Hearing a disorganized commotion suggestive of amateur breakfast preparations, he jumped up with a start. He untangled himself from the mosquito net tucked securely under the matttress which lay atop a frame covered with wooden planks. An insistent buzzing nagged at his ear, and he encountered his first mosquito, that tiny insect whose bite is deadlier than that of a lion.

Swat! Missed! Oh, well, one doesn't become an expert mosquito swatter overnight.

He probed for his slippers to avoid contact with the raw concrete floor. He could imagine the identification grooves his bare feet would leave in the dust accumulation. Maybe this government rest house prided itself as the epitome of bush accommodations, but as far as he was concerned, it would take some getting used to.

His three traveling companions, missionaries of varying

degrees, were giving the impression of seasoned safarians. The newcomer followed suit, although in reality, it was little different from the washing-up and open-air eating of his boyhood days on the Missouri farmlands.

"Dr. Miley, how do you like your eggs?" called builder-turned-chef Dan Merkh as he hunched over the portable gasoline camp stove.

Startled at such a request under such surroundings, the missionary-to-be faltered briefly, then answered, "With the white done and the yellow runny." He might have expected something exotic like roasted monkey or creamed crocodile.

"Coming right up!"

Carrying the designated pan to the communal faucet, he splashed his body to attention with the icy water. Shaving would wait until another day. He was suddenly aware of why men were inclined to beards on these inland treks.

Breakfast proved an adventure. Perhaps the bread had once been crusty and crunchy hot from the earthen oven; but the night dampness had sapped it of its spirit, and it, like his mattress, drooped and sagged. He doused the leathery pastry generously with butter and jam and tried not to notice how vigorously he chewed.

A warm spirit of comradeship and oneness in the Spirit united the quartet. Bill Jones and Lonnie Sparks had already established themselves with other tribes in the Bondoukou Circle, but they unanimously agreed that the most primitive tribe of all, the Lobis, might possibly be reached by establishing the medical work among them. Dan Merkh, the mission builder, was available to start construction as soon as plans were finalized.

The doctor thought briefly of his family a continent away. What his camera failed to capture, he mentally photographed in order that they might share this experience. He searched for word pictures to describe the crisp freshness of the early morning air faintly scented with blossoms from the nearby nyime trees, the distant thump-thump of pestles battling the grain in wooden mortars, the not-too-distant babble of voices chanting an intonation the like of which he had never heard before.

The village was stirring to life. In no time at all small black faces took up vantage points to stare in unashamed curiosity. It seemed he wasn't the only one taking mental pictures. He felt a peculiar kinship to the zoo animals. He acknowledged the presence of these little ones and continued his performances of drying the dishes, packing up belongings, and loading the *Volkswagen*.

He hadn't yet even caught a glimpse of the Lobis, the tribe he had crossed the Saharas to find. However, their reputation preceded them. Savages. Beasts. Primitives. These, his Lobis. His heart burned within him at the mere mention of the name. Leaving Bouna and following the deeply grooved dirt road northward toward the Upper Volta border, they entered the fringe of Lobi Land.

The wandering missionaries were directed to a Lobi funeral in full swing. The bus left the main road and bounced over the rutted cow path until the indistinct route blended with the burned-off countryside. The guide gestured to stop and said something which could only be interpreted to mean, "Now we walk."

Locking their provisions in the car and taking only cameras, they followed single file along the winding path, weaving a trail around trees, skirting fields, through a dried up river bed. Silently, briskly, they loped along the unfamiliar path.

Gradually they were aware of a vague, alien sound just ahead, increasing in volume and intensity with each step. Soon the air filled with a syncopation of cries, wailing, drumbeats, and periodic blasts from what sounded like a miniature cannon.

They came over a rise, and a scene from another world leaped out before them. The sight so indelibly engraved upon his memory that he was sure it would remain with him for as long as he lived. They stood frozen, transfixed.

A lone tree, bare and unimpressive, was center stage of this vast arena. A cloud of stifling gray dust enveloped the area, obscuring even the bright noonday sun. The very ground seemed to respond to the beat of the many dancers vibrating, circling the tree like a carnival carousel in slow motion. The female dancers were naked except for clusters of waxy leaves attached to their hip beads. The men wore arm and ankle bands of cowrie shells and headbands decorated with chicken feathers.

The missionaries moved in, close to each other, as if to borrow courage one from the other.

The corpse was tied in a sitting position at the base of the tree. He had been a handsome young man in life, but now appeared almost macabre in death with his legs stretched before him, hands folded in his lap, and dried blood splotching his nose and mouth. Or was it all dried? The doctor almost imagined some of the blood to be fresh and strained for a closer look. A half-gourd covered his semi-bent head. Farther above, a nearly drained sacrificial chicken dripped her squeezed out driblets, ker-plop, ker-plop, to the spectacle below.

The music section was manned by a huge specimen of muscle and brawn who beat the goat-skin covered drum in perfect rhythm with the beat of the balafon. A cripple sat on a low seat before this xylophone-type instrument producing bell-like music with his two padded sticks. Every now and then someone would toss a handful of cowrie shells to the musicians until the ground around them resembled a pebbled patio.

The old and feeble women grouped about the corpse, shooing away the flies which made a constant attack on the decaying body. Occasionally their voices would lift in a weak wail, reminiscent of the days when they once were young and supple and danced untiringly about the tree.

The missionaries stood in speechless speculation. In a moment of time they had been, as it were, transported to Satan's abode. The atmosphere fairly crackled with demonic power.

Something alerted his attention behind. It was well he was yet a young man with a strong heart. As he turned, he noticed they were surrounded by a group of older men who stood poised and watchful, their bows and poisoned arrows slung carelessly about their shoulders, only a hand's reach away.

"What have we gotten ourselves into?" the expression on the missionaries' faces spoke in unison. "Nothing but what the Lord who had led them would get them out of," they quickly reassured themselves.

Via interpreter, they conversed with the father of the dead boy. As they searched for words to express sympathy, the initial barrier between himself and the Lobi people began to be bridged. Sorrow is a universal language.

This brief contact with the Lobi people taught him that they were not a hostile people. Remote perhaps, reserved to be sure, but potentially open and friendly. He knew as he turned and made his way back over that winding path that he would return. It was as though he was leaving a part of himself back there in that dusty arena. And in a way he was. It was the promise that someday he would return with the gospel of Light that would turn their world of darkness upside down.

And this he did just 13 months later. But first there was Paris, and his family.

The liner turned and pointed eastward,
Out across the vast Atlantic,
Far from family and relation.
Cut were all the ties that held him.
     While lunch waited, he stood watching.
On the deck he watched and waited,
Til the torch that stood so bravely
Dropped from sight in the horizon.
And he stood there, primed and thoughtful,
     One step closer to the Lobis.

-11-

Parlez-vous Francais?

Paris, France 1960–1961

Enroute to New York where we boarded the S.S. *United States*, we had accumulated odds and ends along the way, pastimes, games, puzzles, and books for the five-day trip. We had planned to arrange these in the parking lot at the dock, but not so. As the director of our mission board drove us up to the pier, we had to unload and move on—pronto! So each of us gathered up an armload of straggling goods and plodded up the gangplank. Our image captured by candid camera indicates we loaded with scowls, not smiles.

The lunch bell sounded just as we drifted out of the New York harbor. LaVerne lingered until the last possible moment to catch the last glimpse of his homeland. As the Statue of Liberty drifted out of sight, her torch lifted high in the horizon, a lump caught in his throat. Woud he ever see her again? Would he ever return to his homeland? So quickly had childhood passed to adulthood, and now he sensed a greater adventure just ahead. The river was meeting the ocean for the first time, and he stood on the deck of that steamer, reluctant and yet, quite eager.

We stood in awe of that first sea adventure. Being off-season, we were equipped with cabin class facilities (at tourist rates) which included two rooms with private baths, wall-to-wall carpeting, and a spacious elegance we had never known. And the food! Our rare occasions of dining out had been limited to Britling's Cafeteria, so we almost needed an interpreter to translate the eight-course dinners into our understanding. It was well we enjoyed it that first day because the rest of the voyage was unmentionable. I spent most of the time sitting on the bathroom floor with my head hung over the commode. There's no sickness like sea sickness because there's no place you can get away from it. Though we ascended to the highest deck, it was there. If we descended to the lowest chambers, it was there. Darkness and light were both alike. LaVerne and Lynette at least made their appearance at most meals. His thrifty nature reminded him that these meals were paid for so he might as well get the most from them. Often 75 percent of the places would be vacant.

From LeHavre, we took a boat train to Paris. The lush French countryside looked like a picture-book illustration, but we were immersed in sadness to witness the ravages of war—demolished bridges and rails and stacks of blown-out machinery. Yet the green growth enveloping the ruins seemed a promise that even this too would pass.

A representative from Missionary Orientation met us in Paris and deposited us in a hotel to await completion of our apartment. LaVerne will always remember that first taxi ride through the streets of Paris. He had first considered buying a car here, but after witnessing the traffic and the manner of driving, he concluded he wouldn't even feel safe on a bicycle.

L'Avenir Hotel didn't quite measure up to American standards, but we were so excited about being there it didn't matter. We would all feel better after eating, we decided. No one wanted to go out for a big dinner, fearful of attacking a foreign restaurant, language, and customs; so LaVerne and Lynn went to fetch a simple meal. We had joined the ranks of International students—in reverse.

We didn't realize how simple the meal would be. It's still difficult for me to envision my capable husband in the role of shopper that first day. Usually calm, controlled, and well-organized, this has to be his most out-of-character role.

Supermarkets were not found in Paris, especially not in the hotel vicinity. One store sells bread, another meat, another pastry, another fruit and vegetables, and another groceries. Successfully completing one purchase means the procedure has to be repeated in the next store, and so on. English and sign language didn't carry him very far.

"Two," he indicated to the clerk, pointing to some pastry

and holding up two forefingers.

"*Deux?*" the clerk echoed,holding up the thumb and forefinger.

"No, two," he replied, emphasizing the two forefingers. Even sign language was different!

It wasn't over when the clerk finally grasped your meaning. It still had to be paid for.

"*Deux cent francs,*" was the amount to be paid. The clerk waited impatiently while he frantically rummaged through his change, trying to decifer the faded engraving. A line began to form behind him. The clerk's patience changes to exasperation. Finally in total helplessness, he handed over all his currency and indicated she take what she wanted.

Father and son looked so forlorn as they entered that hotel room. Potato chips, hard bread, and apple turnovers were the best they could manage. We found some water in the bathroom to wash it down with. We learned it wasn't stale bread at all; all French bread tastes that way after a few hours. Bread is baked several times daily; and hot from the oven, there's just nothing better, according to our children, than that warm, crunchy goodness.

One of the sub-standard qualities of the hotel was the lack of heat. Finally, even though in the middle of the day, we all piled in bed under covers to get warm and slept until supper time.

That evening we still weren't up to a venture of the city, and Lynn wasn't too eager to venture forth again, so Larry accompanied Daddy in search of food. By this time he had the money system down pat and a French-English dictionary in his pocket.

A smiling pair returned this second time. I was reminded of Isaac who sent his son to find food. When Jacob returned to his father with meat, Isaac inquired, "How is it that you have found it so quickly, my son?" Whereupon Jacob replies, "The Lord God brought it to me."

This bespoke our sentiments as we viewed the *Ritz* crackers, cheese, and real *Coca Colas*. We found this latter product to precede us everywhere we went, even deep in the African bush.

We both enrolled in the Alliance Francaise to study French. Before leaving for France, someone asked, "What language will you speak in Africa?" A classic answer of an ignorant missionary candidate followed, "Well," I began knowingly, "we will speak Lobi, but first we'll have to learn French because Lobi is a French dialect. Besides, they say French isn't very hard."

Nothing could be further from the truth. The Lobi language is not related to French in any manner. Because Ivory Coast had only recently gained her independence from France and all government business as well as schools and commerce were in French, we were required to know this basic language. I don't know who the "they" were who said French wasn't hard. It is well the understatement of all times. French *was* hard.

We boarded the metro and made our way to the Alliance Francaise for this first day in French class. With the help of someone who spoke English, we were directed to a room upstairs where students were being screened for placement in the various classes. We sat down with the others and were handed a paper that we assumed evaluated our knowledge of French.

I couldn't even read where to write my name. An inbred sense of honesty restricted me to look at another's paper during a test, but desperation overruled conviction. I sneaked a glance at my husband's paper, and it was just as blank as mine. "What are we going to do?" I panicked. I signed my name the same place on the paper as he did and handed them to the director. We were immediately placed in the class for pre-schoolers.

The former Greek professor took to language study like a duck to water. In no time he had left me far behind because a pupil moves at his own speed with monthly exams given to rate your progress. You score well, you move to the next level. After nine months he completed the oral requirements for his certificate and enrolled at the School of Tropical Medicine for a three-month study of our expected tropical diseases.

He had grown accustomed to Alliance teachers who spoke with careful diction and exact intonation. Now he was being taught by teachers who muffled their French around a cigarette. He did manage to earn his certificate, and with these two added to his others, he felt he was ready, at least academically, for Africa.

Our second sea voyage was all a sea voyage should be. The last week of our trip we hugged the African continent and basked in the tropical breezes and planned excitedly for the days just ahead.

His life had been a giant kaleidoscope. Almost every year the instrument had given a complete turn; and events, circumstances, people, and lessons learned produced a clear-cut and purposeful design. Now the bits and pieces were shuffling again. Instinctively he knew that the most explosive design of all was about to burst into view. His life among the Lobis was just around the next bend.

PART III
EARLY YEARS IN LOBI LAND

On his schedule he had planned it—
Do "this" first, then "that" will follow.
But his people, this not knowing,
Brought their sick ones prematurely.
"I'm not ready!"
                    But he took them,
Working with the Great Physician—
He the treating; God, the healing.
He could ask no better method
In his work among the Lobis.

-12-

Venom, Vitamins, And Victory!

Doropo Station 1962

Those first months on the Doropo station were one continual frustration. How could he convince the people he wasn't ready to treat patients? Some were sick, critically so, and his heart went out to them. But many were like a few Americans—and his heart also went out to them—they responded to a little sympathy, a listening ear, a bandage, aspirin, or ear drops.

A man walked 25 miles bringing his sick boy with a message from the local school teacher. The note asked the white medicine man to "restore the boy to health." They located the doctor stretching barbed wire at the far end of the property. The child must have been about 11 or 12, but his skinny frame resembled a child half that age. His dull and listless eyes gazed at the man in whom he had placed all his hope.

With great difficulty, the doctor put on the broken record— the clinic wasn't finished, the fence and other buildings occupied his time, he had no medicines, etc., etc.

The child's father listened patiently, almost with an air of detachment. When the doctor stopped, the father proceeded to state in elaborate terms how glad he was to meet the fine doctor from America of whom everyone spoke so highly. Weren't they fortunate he had come to live among them?

This simple bush man could have taught Dale Carnegie something about winning friends and influencing people. Who said flattery would get you nowhere? Besides, the doctor reasoned—to himself and others should they care to ask—the reputation of America was at stake.

The fence work halted while he installed a makeshift lab on the dining room table. An examination revealed a tropical parasitic infection. The doctor fixed him up with what he had and sent him on his way, trusting the Lord to do the rest and restore him to health.

In those days he made an agreement with the village nurse to care for the sick. If the case was beyond his means, he'd write a note to the doctor and send it along with the patient. Hopefully, only these special patients were ministered to.

Manakhir, the Old Chief's daughter-in-law, came to have her large leg ulcer dressed. He carefully explained that the village nurse would care for it, that he only saw those whom the nurse sent with instructions. She was quite impressed with this paper deal and hung around to watch how it worked.

A few days later she returned bearing her "instructions" from the nurse. At least she had picked up a scrap of paper from somewhere and to her, one piece of paper was just as good as another.

The trust and simplicity of the people humbled him. They came to him with medical problems that would baffle even the specialists. The human body seemed to be a stage on which a whole orchestra of physical operations was performed—piercing of ears, as well as the upper and lower lips, scarring of face and umbilical region, chipping and extracting teeth, female circumcision and shaving of hair.

The general surgeon could have a heydey in Africa, especially if he specializes in herniorrhaphies. These invariable masses of many years duration often extended to the patient's knees. Although the African inherited a congenital weakness, this condition is aggravated by the tremendous loads that are carried.

He was not ready to tackle hernias. Even the simple slit leg almost threw him for a loop.

An elderly man toppled from a bicycle, neatly slashing his calf. Hearing of the white medicine man at a nearby village, he brought his problem to the medical team consisting of the doctor and his non-professional assistant, his wife.

Later the doctor learned to delight in such simple cases because he had his share of genuine frustrations. Questionable cases in which he'd give almost anything for a professional consultation, surgical cases turned away because of lack of equipment and personnel, patients requiring unavailable treatment, no proper medication–these often bring a deep weariness. But give the doctor a mangled hand to treat, and he perks up like a child with a new toy. Here he is master. Though the procedure may often be routine, the results are dramatically visible.

But he was far from master of this situation because the unestablished medical center was only lines on the architect's drawing board. He brought in a bench and seated the patient on the unscreened back porch. He began to scrounge around for functional equipment—straight sewing needle and thread, eyebrow tweezers, manicure scissors, cosmetic cotton, and rubbing alcohol. Needless to say, the suturing process didn't operate too smoothly either. The miniature tweeezers slid over the skin, the scissors chewed the thread, and the needle refused to follow the doctor's instructions to curve. To top it all, the skin persistently gaped like the hole in an overgrown boy's pants.

I ached in pity for him and sympathetically offered, "Here, let me help you." Carefully placing both hands on either side of the wound, I held it securely together, then looked up for his approval.

The doctor froze in disbelief, jaw gaped, and eyes registering blind shock. At last he spoke. "You're not sterile!"

My thoughts raced. "Who? Me!" "Not sterile?" "On this messy, unscreened porch?" "Chicken and flies everywhere?" The patient, clad in clothes that most likely had never seen water, lay prostrate on a dirty cement floor.

And the doctor feared *my* unsterile hands.

However, he did appreciate my help (after I returned from washing) and ended up with a neat closure which healed nicely. It survived a slight infection though which he observed with glee. It served as an object lesson to anyone daring to assist in surgery with unsterile hands.

He often called on his non-professional assistant whenever a procedure required help, but I learned to respect the doctor's territory. I became quite expert in running errands, swatting flies, wiping sweat, and fanning, but he could do the suturing very well alone, thank you.

An S.O.S. quickly alerted the States requesting proper suturing equipment. These were duly christened one Sunday morning when a 15 year old boy with a torn scrotum interrupted the morning church service. The doctor cleaned off the carpenter's table under the Nerri Pod tree and performed the repair in an open-air theater. It seemed rather a private procedure for so large a crowd, but no one minded in the least. From one to 60 people always come with a patient anyway. Not always out of sympathy, he learned, but the African has an inbred sense of curiosity. They can watch through your bedroom window and look through your drawers or down your throat with such natural ease that you feel like an old grouch to resent such kindly interest in your affairs.

Even delivering a baby seemed almost a public exhibition. Obstetrics was not his choice of the specialities, but he quickly discovered it to be the most demanding. The tribal midwives had always delivered their own babies and no doubt would continue to do normal deliveries for as long as time. Some babies lived and some died. If they weren't born dead, they often died soon after. He supposed half of all babies born actually grew to adulthood. Tetanus, malaria, victims of diseased parents, measles, improper care, malnutrition, and accidents contributed to this speculation.

His first OB case was a woman in her fourth pregnancy. In her eighth month she went into labor. After one arm was delivered, her pains stopped and she was left to die along with her unborn child. The school teacher suggested they try the new white doctor.

"Only a miracle will save her," the doctor predicted after his initial visit. One day he would be able to accept these cases with a certain degree of confidence, but today all he could think of was the desperate lack of all to which he had been accustomed. Total absence of a clean room, sterile equipment, adequate instruments, and trained help. Sure, he had a wife who could do urine and blood and stool analyses, but that's a far cry from a surgical assistant. He rubbed his thumb over the ends of his fingers, and

104

Dr. Miley preaching
Disoumte (Kontin Paul)
in the background

Patients waiting in front of clinic

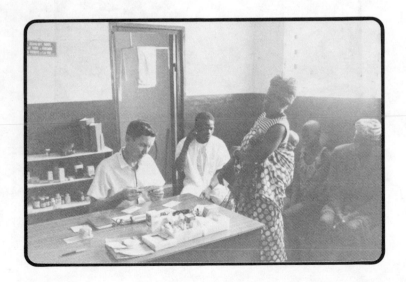

Dr. Miley and patients

Dr. Miley baptizing Mousa

Brush arbor during youth camp

Lobi funeral dance

having a rough edge, began to chew. Some day perhaps there would be the where-with-all, but what about *now*? *Today* a woman is dying.

Like an answer to prayer, he remembered a box of instruments—old, rusted, out-moded, given him by Dr. Keith, his benefactor through medical school. Had he listened to his wife, they would never have taken the space to come. He located them in a barrel and brought them forth as buried treasure. After scouring them thoroughly, he immersed them in boiling water.

While the instruments boiled, he placed other essentials in a cardboard box. Committing it all to the Lord—what he had to work with and whom he had to help him—he said, "Let's go."

We made our way to the village and into that small windowless hut where the tiny woman lay on a bloody rag spread on a pure dirt floor. A small fire glowing to one side raised the temperature to a high pitch. Curious bystanders and interested family and midwives filled every available inch of space. The room reeked of sweat, smoke, blood, and urine.

"Who is the mother?" the doctor asked, looking around the group. When several volunteered, he realized "mother" is a broad term, so he chose two capable-looking women to help. "The rest of you wait outside," he ordered with a nod toward the tiny entrance way. They didn't want to but they were afraid not to.

The doctor learned something that afternoon that he observed many times since. The pain tolerance of the Lobi people, especially the women, is unbelievably high. Suffering is a part of their existence, and they accept it in the same manner as they accept hunger, thirst, heat, and cold.

As the doctor knelt, crunching the knees of his white trousers in the dirt, he began unwrapping the pitiful instruments. It was my first delivery by decapitation (my first delivery period), and later, in retrospect, I marveled I took it so well. I was becoming quite an expert—I wiped sweat before it dripped into his area of work, chased flies away before they lit, and properly manipulated the flashlight to coincide with the movement of the instruments.

He hadn't even returned home when the government nurse

105

met him asking him to come quickly and see another OB patient at his dispensary.

"Sounds like she needs a Caesarean section," he mused at the nurse's description.

"The box of instruments may have helped in one emergency; would they be adequate for another?" It did include forceps. At least you can't send someone home to die until you have exhausted every human resource.

Family and friends milled through the courtyard. Via an interpreter, the doctor explained the gravity of the situation. He could try forceps. A low murmur spread over the crowd . . . louder . . . louder . . . then it reached palaver level . . . on and on. The newcomer could not understand the words tossed back and forth, but he needed no translator to understand the tone which implied many were not in favor of this thing suggested by the white doctor. Iron hands to penetrate the birth canal? Hun-un! (No way!)

Some day there would be adequate facilities to properly care for these patients, but long before then, people in Lobi Land would trust their women into the hands of this man who cared for them as tenderly as he did his own family. For the time being, he thanked God that at least one woman was alive who might have died. She was bereaved of this child she had not yet learned to love, but he stayed there long enough to fill those empty arms with other children from her womb.

It became more and more evident that our unscreened back porch and the shade of the Nerri Pod tree were inadequate hospital pavilions. Too, a job was hardly begun and carried through to completion without an interruption or two from sick folks demanding attention. The clinic was still months away from completion.

"There's our empty trailer over there," suggested Dan Merkh. "It's not much, only one room, but at least you can have a place to treat the sick in privacy."

A coat of white paint transformed the interior to an authentic examining/treatment room. In no time at all, a regular schedule of treating patients was established.

As they gathered under the shade tree, they were given a

106

block of wood on which a number was painted and were treated in that order. Some days those blocks would change hands several times as up to 200 patients were treated.

Tetanus was among the most terrifying illnesses he treated in that makeshift clinic.

Because tetanus (lockjaw) is included in childhood injections, one rarely sees this disease in the States. Still, statistics reveal over 60 percent of tetanus patients in the United States hospitals die in spite of top-notch care and medication. His first experience with this killer was a terrifying, heart-wrenching one.

The doctor stood on the porch and watched him coming up the path to the house, that stumbling boy about 16 years of age, clad only in dirty shorts. Another man hovered helplessly beside him, helping only when he fell. Their short journey was often punctuated by these convulsive spasms in the dirt. It seemed an eternity before he reached the porch.

The man told his story. They lived in a town up north across the border, but for some time they had worked down south. When this sickness attacked the boy, they went to the government dispensary only to be told there was no cure. They caught the first truck coming up country. Enroute a fellow passenger told them of the new doctor in Doropo, so they persuaded the driver to drop them off here.

The history was interrupted from time to time by the boy's spasms. A sudden noise, a raised voice, or a short movement would trigger a convulsion. His teeth clenched, back arched, gasping for air, he'd undergo about 20 seconds of unadulterated agony.

We had no antitetanus vaccine, but the antitoxin neutralizes the poison not yet fixed in the central nervous system, and it was evident the poison had anchored through his body. A tranquilizer, a muscle relaxant, and a prayer—this was all he had to send him on his way. Next day he learned the duet had caught another truck in the night for the final lap of their journey.

Never were the other experiences with tetanus as terrifying as this first one, but no less tragic. The next one grieved him because it struck one of his favorite patients. Doctors do have favorites, you know. An exploding gun pumped rocks and gunpowder into the foot of this 14 year old boy causing extensive damage.

The clinic still wasn't open, so available treatment consisted of soap, water, and clean rags. The doctor dug out rocks and debris, sutured the various holes, and willed the foot to heal. The family took up lodging across the road, and the doctor made daily house calls.

Twice the healing was interrupted by gouging out more rock. Once it looked like gangrene was setting in and the doctor suggested an unheard of course of treatment—amputation. Nothing doing!

Our sheet bandages were limited, so he issued two. Each day the family would have the discarded one washed and dried for re-dressing. He left soap and each day the wound was cleansed thoroughly before he arrived. One day the family marveled at how well the foot was healing and was quick to rebuke the doctor, "And to think, you wanted to chop it off!"

Their village was some distance, and with the danger seemingly past, they became restless to return. When their impatience could not be stilled, the doctor issued detailed instructions for his care and let him go.

A few weeks later the boy's father returned describing the boy's turn for the worse. He didn't know, neither did we, that that young boy with the quick, smiling eyes, expansive sharp-pointed teeth, and full with the promise of life was marked for death. Not only gravel and dirt had exploded in his foot, but tetanus germs had been breeding all the while.

He had few words of common language, yet felt much that did not need to be spoken. Some emotions are so delicate they are threatened to be shattered by speech.

Never again to our knowledge did he lose a patient from lack of antitetanus medication. Twice our curative supply was inadequate, so we sent the patient elsewhere where she received massive doses, but it was too late. The other left with nothing more than a couple of initial injections, but he lived. Yes, many, many times the Great Physician took over and healed in spite of, or because of, his inadequacies those years in Africa.

When we arrived in Africa, we considered identifying with

our people in matters of housing, living, food, and dress. After all, a good missionary is one who totally identifies with his people, we were told. One look at the situation produced second thoughts. It would be impossible and still be physically fit to do the work he had come to do. The Lobis had built up a certain amount of resistance to many of the diseases, and while they did perhaps have a natural insecticide and netting about their bodies, we observed that many had long forgotten what it's like to feel well.

That first month in Africa, the rains had stopped several months before and the wells dried up, stream beds parched and rivers were dangerously low. Our water came from a non-running stream, the same water in which cows refreshed themselves, lepers bathed, and women did their laundry. Do you wonder why we tried to reach the stream first in the morning?

Even so, we boiled and filtered every drop we drank. Later with our reservoirs of clear rain water and wells of fresh, sparkling water, we still followed this procedure. Water preparation loomed as the biggest single chore on the mission field— keeping enough water filtered, boiled, and cooled in sufficient amounts for family use and unexpected guests.

The doctor bordered on the fanatical when he first went to Africa. One evening the family sat down to a supper of packaged soup. He raised to dip in and—would you believe it?—so did a bug attracted by the Aladdin lamp. There must be something about his body chemistry—if there's one fly in the house, it'll swarm over his plate; if there's one mosquito around, he's going to be the one bitten; if one stray bug escapes the flour sifter, it's going to be in his piece of bread.

Well, he looked at that bowl of soup in disgust. "There's a bug in my soup," was the nearest curse he could muster.

He's not a finicky eater. He married a girl whose chief past time was trying out new recipes, and he'd brave them all in the name of love. Never before had he been threatened with food contaminated by varmints.

He wasn't about to eat it, you could tell. He's not overly fond of packaged soups anyway. "Can't you just pick him out?" the cook implored. There was neither soup nor anything else prepared, and the nearest grocery store hundreds of miles away.

109

(She, too, was adjusting to this new living arrangement.) He answered by scooting back his chair and asking to be excused.

It took a year. But one day he became Africanized.

In mid-dry season, he journeyed over a hot dusty road in Upper Volta. At long last, parched and weary, he arrived for a rest stop at a mission station. As custom, he was served a tall, cold glass of lime-aid pressed from limes grown right on the compound. There's nothing more refreshing to him than lime-aid. Just as there are Coke addicts in Africa, his addiction is to this tart drink.

His jaws ached in anticipation as the ice clinked invitingly with each swirling movement. Then he saw it. A tiny bug squirmed right on top. He tried to drink around him. He rotated his glass in this direction, then that, hoping to spill him out. The bug which refused to either sink or spill, seemed to be drawn to the lips as a magnet. Okay. It's either the lime-aid *and* the bug or no lime-aid at all. In one gulp, he was gone.

He didn't choke, he reported later. But had a camera caught his expression in that moment of swallowing, it would surely have been akin to that of his patients when they experience their first taste of castor oil.

The doctor's fanaticism didn't diminish when it came to washing his hands. One observer comments, "I'm surprised he has any skin left on his hands, the way he washes them."

Another remarked, "He touches each of his patients—and then goes and washes his hands." Although a slight exaggeration, it is a habit you don't miss. In the clinic plans, he allowed for a lavatory just off the doctor's office.

The family sits at the table waiting for the head of the house to take his place.

"Here comes Daddy," one of the children calls and Mama pours the iced tea .

He enters the house and walks to the bathroom. Twenty-one steps. Now he may have washed his hands just before leaving the clinic, but that doesn't suffice for now. He walks to the table. Seventeen more steps.

Often the meal is interrupted at some point with a "Caw Caw" or the slap of hands or the call "Monsieur."

110

He rises to answer the call. Twelve steps.

A handshake is just as common as a hello, so probably a physical contact has been made. Maybe not. In either case, business transacted, he feels contaminated, thus another washing before continuing the meal. Twenty-one steps to the bathroom. Seventeen back to the table.

Is it any wonder he lost weight on the mission field?

"Love your wife," he told them plainly,
And they watched him for their know-how.
"Love your children," and he showed them
As they lived and worked among them.
"Love the God, the One who loves you
Gave His Son for your redemption."
This God? Yes, His name is Thangba,
Though we thought he'd gone and left us.
By His Spirit, He indwells us.
He was ever an example
To His people, to his Lobis.

–13–

All In The Family

Children and Vacations

Separation from the children for long periods of time became the hardest adjustment to make on the mission field. We could have continued to teach them by Calvert correspondence-Larry was finishing grade three, Lynette, grade six, and Lynn, grade eight. The two older ones missed companionship and competition while the younger lacked the discipline to work on his own. One had to fairly tie Larry to his seat in order for him to write his daily composition. Arithmetic and reading he'd fairly sail through, but compositions! At that point the cry of Mother Nature was stronger than the thirst for knowledge.

"Larry, if you don't sit in that chair until your school work is finished, I'm going to . . . ." Every day, every day.

One typical morning—he's older now, in the ninth grade and following the University of Nebraska program—he had sat down to study. The instructions were addressed to him, and his father only acted as supervisor, administering tests, and giving assistance as needed. As usual, before we left for the clinic, his father went over the day's schedule and suggested that "this and this and this" be completed before he took off, as he was prone to do.

Larry spread out his books and papers over the dining room table. This provided a good view of both the front and back of the house and not nearly so confining as the view from his desk in his room. He had just gotten down to work on "this" when the call of a quail broke into his concentration. He tried to ignore that first time, but that second call sounded for all the world like a dare.

He laid aside his books and picked up his gun to accept the

challenge. He lost all consciousness of time as he plunged deeper and deeper into the African bush. One quail called and another echoed. The crisp air brushed clean and cool over his face, and the smell of flowers hung in the air. The fragrant blossoms of the honeysuckle struck his nostrils, and he paused to admire the deep purple of the wild morning glories.

He mentally marked the spot. "I'll come back later and get some seeds," he promised himself. "Mother will want to plant them." He was thoughtful of such things. As he explored further he found some white gravel that would make a pretty patio. "I must tell Mother about this," he thought. All he had seen before were the reddish rocks down on the river bed.

An approaching noise, a very familiar one, coming up just behind him, sent a streak of terror through him. "What time was it anyway?" He glanced at his watch—"Good grief!" "Ten o'clock already!" "Where had the morning gone?" "Was it really *two* hours ago that he left?"

He tracked the sound of the Honda as he approached and came into view. There appeared his white-clad father who had left his work at the busiest hour of the morning to chase down his delinquent son.

"I came over to see if you needed help with your geometry. The houseboy said you'd been gone since 8. What happened?"

"Well," he began apologetically, "there was this quail and . . . . "

It wasn't the first time. Neither would it be the last.

Although we would have chosen to keep them with us, we reluctantly agreed that boarding school had superior advantages over correspondence study.

Lynn had a choice when we arrived in Ivory Coast. He could dilly-dally along with the seventh grade Calvert course and enroll at the Conservative Baptist grade school in Ivory Coast for the eighth grade, along with his sister and brother who were enrolled. Or he could conclude his seventh grade work while we waited for his eighth grade books to arrive from the States. He had four months to finish this grade before enrolling in high school in Mamou, Guinea, a Christian and Missionary Alliance sponsored school almost 1,000 miles away.

114

He'd rather be ahead than behind, so he decided to knuckle down to study. I guided the two younger ones through classes, while LaVerne took Lynn. Although it proved a time-consuming project, it had definite advantages. Lynn developed a good background of English grammar, thus making later courses a snap. But more importantly, he learned to study—how to evaluate the matter before him, select what is important, and how to commit it to memory for recall.

Four hours of concentrated study each morning sufficed to keep him on schedule. Lynette, on the other hand, sat at her desk much of the day. I suspect girls are more inclined to day-dreaming.

D-Day came in mid-July. His newly ordered wardrobe of shirts and pants and socks and underwear arrived from Sears export store in time to be labeled and trunked for school. The plan entailed driving him to Ferke, the Conservative Baptist mission station, there to connect with a truck going after some Mamou graduates.

We drove all day and pulled into the Welch's drive just as dusk fell. The countdown had already started—the loaded truck was primed to leave after a quick meal. Somehow we had thought it would be morning.

We stood in the black African night and watched them gather up their last minute supplies. Our five were shaken, puzzled. We were separating for the first time in our lives and had no past experiences to guide us. Lynn looked so small and helpless, yet so brave as he gestured his farewells and disappeared into the bigness of the truck bed.

"Wait! Wait!" we wanted to call out and grab Time by the coattail. "We're not ready."

The truck passed through the gate and disappeared from sight in the mango grove. Just an hour ago these men had been total strangers, these to whom we had entrusted our 13 year old. "Oh, God, please . . . ."

We met Lynn at the airport when he arrived for Christmas vacation. What had happened to our little boy? He left a child and returned a maturing young man. We could hardly believe that four months could make such a difference. Yet when Larry passed through this stage a few years later, he was home and it seemed we could literally see him grow before our eyes. Growing from babyhood and growing into adulthood have many similarities.

Saying good-bye never gets any easier. One never learns to perform mechanically. Following our first furlough, Lynn graduated from high school and enrolled in our Bible College in Nashville, our alma mater. We had reservations to sail on a freighter leaving New Orleans the first part of August. My parents and Lynn accompanied us and were to return a few days later. That morning, in that guest house for missionaries, they prepared to leave.

It was no easier leaving him at 17 than it had been at 13. I remember thinking, "It's a good thing everything has been said that needs to be said, because it couldn't be said now." We couldn't even pray audibly.

Two years later he came to Africa for a visit. Had I thought the transformation remarkable before, well, you should have seen our young man now. His growth was not so much physical as mental and spiritual. You can't latch apron strings around the likes of that! He had matured into a fine young man. The next time we would see him he would be a married man and expecting his first child with their applications in as missionaries to the Ivory Coast. How could he have done so well without us?

The Conservative Baptists were preparing to open their Ivory Coast Academy in Bouake that fall of 1962. Larry was registered for fourth grade and Lynette for seventh.

Oh, they were so excited! They had never had so many clothes before—two sets of Sunday clothes, five sets of play clothes, five sets of school clothes, a dozen pairs of socks, and that many changes of underwear. With a name label sewed in each garment, including each sock. Each child had his trunk, and for days they filled it with all the things they wanted to take—a candy can filled with candy, favorite toys, books, as well as stamped, addressed envelopes in which to enclose their weekly letters. We didn't dare think of the actual separation, much less talk about it.

This excitement carried over into our arrival at school, locating their rooms and meeting friends. Daddy went with Larry and helped him unpack while I helped Lynette. Just when

116

everyone began to feel a tinge of sadness, the dorm parents asked, "How many of you kids would like to go swimming?"

Of course! They raced back to their rooms for their brand new swimming togs and gathered around the huge rapide (van) which also promised to be an adventure. Our children airily bade us good-bye with hardly a never-you-mind as they located seats and were whisked off to the swimming pool.

Larry had said good-bye with never a backward glance because, of course, he would tell us all about it when he returned. But as soon as the rapide cleared the corner, the parents were instructed to clear the premises before the children returned.

The children returned to a deserted station. This was almost more than Larry's eight-year-old heart could bear. He never quite got over it.

Approaching Bouake from the north, you come over a rise and all of Ivory Coast Academy lies sprawled over a low plain before you. It happened every time—just as we came over that rise, Larry would grab his stomach as an acute pang of nausea hit him. Once he came out for a visit, the threat of Bouake school days forever past, yet as we came over that rise and he saw that familiar scene, he grabbed his stomach and wailed, "Oh, I feel sick." Perhaps he would still experience it today.

Not long after our arrival in Africa, the head of the house sent a tape back home to our churches. Concerning the children, he said, "Several years ago when we left the States, my wife and I knew something of what to expect on the mission field here in Africa. And one of the hardest to face was the thought of separation from our three children. Now it has become a reality—Lynn some 999 miles from home, Lynette and Larry about 300 miles away—all growing up away from home. All three children getting to be together only about six weeks during the past year. Oh, how much we would like to be near at times just to counsel and encourage them during these all important childhood years when their lives are being molded for the future. Many a time during the night I've found myself kneeling by our bedside or kneeling successively at the foot of three empty beds, asking the Lord to watch over our dear children and recommitting them to His care."

117

However, no one need weep for the "underprivileged" missionary children in Africa. This country is a giant toy box bulging with an inexhaustible supply of playthings. When a child tires of one thing, he can find another just for the taking. Lynette was so pet-attuned that she never wearied of the variety of animals offered.

Our neighbors soon learned of her affinity for animals and brought a continuous stream of helpless creatures to our door. Lynette learned by bitter experience that baby deer and rabbits do not adapt to an unnatural habitat, but that didn't weaken her conviction that "maybe this time it will."

Her menagerie varied and covered the scope of the station. Al, the owl, lived for many years in the limbs of the backyard Nerri Pod tree. Her baby python snubbed his special cage, and when he rejected her frogs and lizards as well, she set him free. Cats abounded, full and free. The faster they multiplied, the happier she was and stubborn about parting with any of them. When some of the Africans begged for them, she suspicioned (with reason) they wanted them more for a meal than a pet.

We were never without a dog. Rover, alias Nut, was a miserable black and white African mutt, but he was ours—Rover Miley, they called him—and merited, according to Lynette, proper respect and regular nutritious meals. He never won the devotion she gave King, her beautiful black shepherd-collie puppy who died of a broken heart when summer vacation ended and she returned to boarding school. Her father gave him a proper burial under a towering shade tree on our station. Kheri, his replacement, won all her pet love, but even so, before the brown canine grew out of puppyhood, she contracted distemper and died.

Monkeys seem to dote most on alien mothering, and even the tiniest thrive on a bottle and TLC. Lynette raised a trio of these—Pint, Squirt, and Doc. Cobra bites finished the latter two, but Pint was too ornery to be outwitted by this wily serpent. He abused his freedom by committing one misdemeanor after another, as eating baby chickens or ravaging the neighbor's cornfield. His life alternated between the cage and freedom.

It was inevitable that such close contact with untamed

wildlife would provide more than just a lot of fun. Twice we made the near-1,000 mile round trip for rabies shots.

One night we pulled into our station following that second trip out for shots. As we busily unloaded the *Volkswagen*, we were unaware of Lynette's business transaction. I stepped into the dimly lit garage and almost bumped into her coming from the opposite direction.

"Look," she whispered in awe, stroking a rat-sized animal resembling a miniature kangaroo. "Just what I've always wanted."

"What is it?"

"A bush baby. You know I've always wanted one."

"What hasn't she always wanted?" I thought.

Her father didn't share her enthusiasm. He couldn't believe his eyes as he squinted at her through the Aladdin-lit darkness.

"Lynette, you get rid of that thing," he ordered. The little feller must have smelled fear or anger or a combination of both. Anyway he set up a thrashing and snapping that startled even his new master.

Daddy didn't say it, but he could have—that her stomach was still sore from her last shot barely 48 hours old, and it's from such wild creatures as this that rabies can come.

"Lynette, you get rid of that thing," he repeated then continued his unloading, thus terminating the matter.

She stooped and very reluctantly, even tearfully, freed this thing she had always wanted.

Her daddy wasn't an old meanie. He really liked pets. Jack was his devoted pet dog until he went away to Bible College. That first Christmas he could hardly wait to get back to him, and he mashed the accelerator a little harder in anticipation. "How's Jack?" he asked his parents.

Old Jack was dead, his parents told him. He must have gotten in some rat poison. Tears filled his eyes, and he pulled over to the side of the road to pull himself together. What would home be without his dog?

No, he wasn't an animal hater. The vaccinated dogs on the station were special with a special attachment developing for Napoleon. But in his way of thinking, the wild life belonged to the wild.

Although the children were away much of the time, vacations were the times we were together. To nudge a missionary from his routine rut, the mission board grants a vacation bonus. To qualify, he must be away from his station on a bonafide vacation. That first term offered small choices, usually a vacant mission station.

Surprisingly enough, the least enjoyable were those spent in Abidjan, the cultural, industrial and sports center of West Africa. Modern supermarkets, ice skating, bowling, swimming, lovely beaches, snack shop with hamburgers and banana splits, Parisienne shops, museums, and even a free modern guest house available—these offer everything for the perfect vacation. But invariably these trips turn out to be unhurried business and shopping trips. When one makes a business trip to Abidjan, the doctor learned to allow time. These little sallies were murder on his fingernails. The three-hour lunch break when everything shuts up tight sliced right through a massive agenda.

Once it took four trips to get his driver's license renewed, three to simply pick up a form to renew Lynn's visa to Guinea, six bookstores before finding the book the African teacher ordered, two hours to get a bill straightened out, seven visits to the customs office to get a necessary paper, not to mention the put-you-offs of getting the car repaired.

Before our guest house was built and we patronized hotels, time was a premium. Lynn once said, "When I get rich, I'm going to see that you have enough money to come to Abidjan without having to be in such a hurry to leave."

On the day we hoped to leave, we'd check out at 12, lug our baggage to the lobby while one of us hung around as guard until stores closed that evening, and hopefully, we would be able to start up country to our first mission station, Koun, about five hours away.

Abidjan vacations allow plenty of time for reading (which *he* doesn't enjoy) and cleaning, repairing and odd jobs (which I don't especially enjoy). These little diversions fall into his idea of recreation. Cleaning and waxing the car leaves him just as fulfilled as a top golf score. He's a museum guide's delight. He scrutinizes every object, doesn't miss a word of the printed text and hangs on to each word.

Two of our most memorable vacations that first term were spent in the mountains of Guinea when our children were enrolled in the high school there. Their schedule was arranged to allow one yearly three-month vacation at Christmas time and a month in July between terms. The children made the 2,000 mile round trip at Christmas, but in July, many of the parents went to their children.

Communistic influence was felt in Guinea even at this time, so all provisions had to be carried in. For these trips we loaded our *Volkswagen* bus with camping equipment, food to last a month—and once, our houseboy—and took off for Bobo Dioulasso, a Christian and Missionary Alliance mission station in Upper Volta. Here we joined with a three- to five-car caravan of other missionaries crossing Communistic Mali bound for the same destination.

Evidently the Malians mistrusted each other, for we hardly got moving well when a road check would loom in front of us. A thorough search through suitcases, cases of food, eggs, the stamp collection. Sometimes we'd hardly move more than 100 yards when the whole procedure would be repeated.

It's wise to travel with a very flexible schedule, else you're bound to wind up with ulcers or some other tension-related illness. Like the wait at the river when the ferry is on the other side and the patron reluctant to acknowledge the persistent honks. Or a washed-out bridge. Or the construction of a passable route.

Ah, yes, these experiences contributed in making him a patient man. He brought his restless impatience to the tropics and collided with the composure and patience of the African. In time he learned to conform. Actually these delays were refreshing interludes. Time to get in a quick game of password, a communal coffee/water break, or more pressing, rearranging the load which was constantly shifting.

Kankan, Guinea, spread as an oasis in the midst of a busy, bustling metropolis (African bush standard). Mr. and Mrs. Kurlack, already retired from missionary service, but reluctant to leave their adopted country, had a reputation of hosting the most hospitable mission station in Africa. They provided dormitory-like rooms for the whole caravan as well as *Ivory* soap, plenty of water (unheated, of course), and spanking-clean white towels. After a trip such as ours, it demanded an out-and-out scrubbing from top to bottom, the towels themselves bearing witness to the thoroughness of the job.

The cleansing stint finished, we filed into a large dining room where a hot meal was served, French style, beginning with soup and ending with fruit. Ah, but it was elegant; it was. Once Mrs. Kurlack even served homemade ice cream.

Although Kankan was the most hospitable, it was the noisiest station of all. An African discotheque blared its pulsating beat just a few feet from our bedroom window, continuing until dawn, the only lull being the changing of the records. Just as the pagans bedded down, the Muslims awoke to activity. On the opposite corner, the mussein ascended the prayer tower and encanted the city to prayer. He towered just above us, so near we imagined we could hear him clear his throat. LaVerne jumped up and grabbed his tape recorder to capture this verbal spectacle, so sleep eluded us that night.

The next morning we completed the last leg of our four-day journey. After a quick stop at the school to hug our children whom we hadn't seen in four months, we continued 40 miles beyond to the mountains of Dalaba. We climbed the steep hillside and received our house assignment from among the 17 homes spread over three different levels. These homes had all been built and were owned by individual missionaries, but if the owners were not occupying them at that particular time, they shared them with others. Some were more elaborate than others. Two actually had indoor plumbing and a few had fireplaces. For the most part they were unfinished shells with doors and windows, with one mud-thatched roof hut among them.

We unloaded our gear, set up and made beds, decided in which room to put the kitchen, and prepared for the arrival of the children the following day. We got our bearings—the spring was up the hill over there, the outside toilet over in that direction, down there was the volley ball court, and the houseboys slept over that-away.

The inconvenience of the place (it wasn't chosen for comfort as we had more comforts at home) was soon overruled by the fellowship that existed among the missionaries. The doughnut party and Jewish auction at chef Nehlsons, sloppy joes and Life game at the Cheddars, stamps and Scrabble with the Watkins, the outdoor pizza parties, picnics and Perquacky at the Pines, the Rocks, the Big Tree, even the worship services with testimonies and tapes, prayer meetings—these all form a composite picture of never-to-be-relived experiences.

One day at the Rocks, Janice Tyler, a teenage friend of Lynette's, fell gashing her forehead. The doctor came unprepared for these emergencies, so he borrowed the bare necessities from a Polish doctor in town. The doctor was especially concerned it turn out well because girls especially are concerned about any facial disfigurement. Janice later returned to college in the States. That first year she fell from horseback, and the Lord took her home to be with Him. Now, praise the Lord, Janice is permanently free from all imperfections.

Even in Guinea, away from all station responsibilities, he felt guilty being idle. Reading is not his idea of enjoyment. Some friends kept up our *Reader's Digest* subscription our whole time in Africa, and he usually browses through it, choosing to read the book-length selection first. Maybe he thinks this compensates for his lack of reading full-length editions. His reading standards are rigid. If it teaches you something or makes you a better person, it's fit to read.

How can someone read for sheer pastime? Occasionally I'd pick up a "best-seller." He'd read the introduction and a few of the front pages, then the ending, browse through the middle, and snap, it's finished. In those few minutes, if there's one word of profanity or a scene the author should have omitted, he's sure to find it. Then I'd receive a few choice words on appropriate reading material for the mature Christian.

"Do you really think you should read a book like that?" he'd begin cautiously.

"But it isn't all like that," I'd defend. "Matter of fact, it's the

123

only page. The plot is good and it's well-written. How you can always manage to spot that one objectionable part is beyond me."

I'm the first to admit some books should be torn to shreds and cremated on the ash heap (as we've done with several books given us). Once I burned some before Larry could see them, and he burned some before I could see them. But the man-of-the-house says, "I've never had drinking or smoking in our home. I've tried to control TV, conversation, and radio programs. I don't intend to have filthy trash around either. A person can't help but be influenced by what he reads."

Although he is not an avid reader, he is well aware of the power of the printed page and often selects books as gifts. At Christmas, the children expected books chosen especially for them, usually dealing with specific problems, devotionals, or helps in Christian living.

At the end of one furlough, we were sorting and packing books. Larry helped me and we were careful to see that none of my parent's books slipped in with ours. Larry held up one he didn't remember. "How to Know The Will of God for Your Life," he read the title. "Is this ours?" Opening the fly leaf, he answered his own question. "It is. It looks like something Daddy would give me."

The time passed quickly in that secluded mountain spot. The day came when the repaired *Volkswagen* was readied for the homeward trip. The children had returned to school, and an air of desertion settled among the pines. Never this side of Heaven would we meet with those same missionaries again. Neither would we see Dalaba again. After our second vacation, the Communists took control and the border clamped shut. Lynette had to be flown out for her final trip.

The years passed quickly, oft unheeded
Two years soon had more than doubled.
    He had dwelt among the Lobis,
Healed their sick and birthed their babies,
Saw them turn to light from darkness.
    "The time has come to make a journey,
    I must needs go see my family."
Thus he told them, almost weeping.
    "Watch for me, you'll see me coming,
    When my furlough time is ended;
    Watch for me, I'll come returning."
Saying thus, he left the Lobis.

–14–

Centre Medical de la Mission Protestante

The Medical Station Opens Its Doors
1963–1965

January 1, 1963 marked a historical day in Free Will Baptist missions. On that day the Centre Medical de la Mission Protestante officially opened her doors for the first time. Months, yea, years had gone into the preparation.

A few weeks previously we journeyed to Upper Volta to record messages in both Lobi and Djula, the two prominent languages in our area. As patients waited for treatment, they could listen to these messages from God's Word, and He could reveal to them what our actions were trying to convey: God loved them, and we had come to dwell among them to demonstrate that love.

Lynn's small rectangular aluminum plaques had been stamped with the number 63 (the year) and beginning with 63-1 and going straight through, plaques were issued as the patients registered. Before the year ended, more than 6,000 of these identification markers were given. Numbers on the plaques matched a card which listed name and age. (Approximately— what African knows his age? We usually underestimated children and youth and overestimated the older ones.)

Each time a patient came, he'd present a plaque, the desk boy would pull his card, date it, and collect his 2¢ visit payment.

It wasn't easy to decide to charge for visits. It didn't take a second look to realize we were living among poor folks. What we considered the basic necessities—food, clothing, and shelter—

126

were woefully lacking or completely absent. How could we with a clear conscience expect to squeeze 2¢ from them when that single act meant they'd have less food to put in the pot? Besides our people in the States were generous, the mission board sympathetic. They would respond to a program of charity.

While Christ commanded charity, doling out gifts is not charity. Often it is a disguised form of racial superiority, and even missionaries are not above this type of prejudice. Yes, his Lobi people would accept his gift, but in time come to despise the giver. What we consider kindness is often interpreted as weakness to the pagan. Even primitive peoples can tell by a look in the eye, in the tone of the voice, in a passing remark, or by a careful analysis of one's attitude whether or not he's loved.

In addition to the initial visit, they paid for medication and injections. Of course, if they didn't have it, they were treated as if they did; and large families were given special cuts. But the doctor let me know right away that he was the one to decide on these special privileges.

The little girl peeped shyly around the door frame leading to the bandage room where I wrapped a sore.

"Come in, Gnar," I motioned to her.

She was about five or six years of age, the cutest, plumpest little thing you ever saw. She had endeared herself to us since that day Dabolo brought her to us unconscious with meningitis. We had prayed for her recovery, and now each time we saw her we were reminded of His love and mercy. Today she was shaven-haired and wore only two strands of bright red beads about her hips. Healthier looking than most, she held up her leg with its big sore which needed a dressing.

"Did you pass by the desk with your 2¢?" I asked her, meanwhile getting the peroxide, gauze, and powder at hand.

"Hun-uh," she shook her head.

"But you know, Gnar, everyone must pass by the desk and pay his money before he can be treated."

Silence. Only the ugly sore crying for attention.

This was becoming a problem. You see, I had a list of Privileged People. These certain ones could by-pass the desk and come directly to the bandage room for treatment and be on their way. Now to be among the Privileged People, you had to be a Sweet Young Thing (as was Gnar), have only a tiny sore, attend church or be the offspring of one who did, or simply one who just touched my heart.

When the General Director of the Medical Center became aware of the situation, he called me into his office for a little tete-a-tete. Such a thing could not be done. We could not afford to show favoritism. There was already too much of that shown in a pagan society. If treatment was worth 2¢ for one, it was worth 2¢ for all, even the Sweet Young Things.

I glanced across the hall to the doctor's office. At any moment, I could just see him popping his head into the bandage room.

"Now, Gnar, you know you have to pay your money."

She flung open her hands indicating her penniless condition.

"Do you have chickens at your house?"

"Oo-oo-oo," she nodded.

"Do they lay eggs?"

"Oo-oo-o."

"Tell you what. Run home and bring me a nice fresh egg. I'll give you two cents for it, and you can get your sore dressed."

She smiled widely in agreement and flew out of the room and off down the road.

The hen must not have been too cooperative, for she didn't return until the next morning. But sure enough, she carried a warm, freshly laid egg.

In such manner, many gifts arrive at the clinic—peanuts, eggs, rice, chickens, guineas, corn, yams, etc.

At the beginning, until the people learned better, these were offered as bribes for preferred treatment. They'd pass by the desk all right with their money and have their card pulled. But with 100 people waiting ahead of him, why that meant he'd be there until noon!

So he'd enter the doctor's office by the back entrance. Even if the doctor is in the midst of treating a patient, you can't very well chase off a fellow if he's offering you a gift. Can't very well ignore it if the gift is a squawking fowl either. The donor, with words couched in diplomatic terms and ringing of good cheer, makes his presentation. The doctor turns aside from his patient to accept the gift, pump his hand, and offer his sincere thanks. The patient remains standing, as if to say, "I've done my part, now it's your turn."

"Oh, but this is a fine chicken. How much is it? I will pay you for it."

"Oh, no, Monsieur. It is a gift."

So the handshaking and thanks giving are repeated all over again. Still he stands. Then comes the nitty-gritty. Could he get treated NOW as he has urgent business elsewhere.

Ah, so, it isn't a gift at all. It's a bribe. He often felt like returning the bribe as the poor man slumped from the room. Over the years the bribes dwindled almost to zero, but the gifts still flowed from grateful people.

"Two years ago my daughter almost died. You gave her medicine. Today she is well and has a new baby. I bring you this chicken." Or these yams, this stalk of bananas, or these peanuts. The cast changes, the gift varies, but the plot is the same. The doctor did something no one else could do, and they want to show their appreciation in the only way they know.

The Little Old Lady with the Twinkly Eyes always brought a gift when she came to the clinic. This was our name for her, this wizened stooped lady with the shaven head, alert eyes, and lip disks as big as half dollars. Accustomed to wearing only leaves and beads, she'd wrap a tiny scrap of cloth about her hips those rare market days when she chose to come to the clinic.

Her gifts were small—a few tomatoes, two or three eggs, corn in season, a handful of peanuts, some beans. A different gift each time. How could she remember what she had already brought? Her kindness and thoughtfulness endeared her to the whole clinic staff.

She was fascinated with the "talking machine" (tape recorder) and always asked to hear the Lobi message. Then she would ask questions. Even though her visits were on our busiest days, her questions were carefully answered, and bit by bit, the way of God took hold in her heart.

One day she interrupted the conversation with, "Would you

please come to my village and tell my people these things you've been telling me?"

"Perhaps we can," the doctor half-way promised. But she was not to be brushed aside so easily. "My husband is chief of the village, and he will pay you well if you will come," she urged.

Not that this was an incentive. However her urgency did result in a definite plan to go to her village eight miles away over a sandy, hilly bush path. It wasn't easy to get away. We were alone on a station occupied with treating an average of 150 patients daily six days a week plus emergencies on Sundays. The doctor also conducted one service on Thursday afternoons and two on Sunday which tied up those days. But the pleading voice, "Won't you please come and tell my people the way of God?" haunted him.

Thus he became a circuit-riding preacher, not riding a horse, but first a bicycle and later a *Honda* donated by Harold Montgomery of Tupelo, Mississippi. One Sunday morning after the regular service and before an emergency arose, he pumped up the tires of his bicycle and took off for her village where he was welcomed by more than 100 pagans, most who had never before heard the name of Jesus.

It was a somber moment as he faced these souls condemned to death and dying in that condition and yet never once hearing that a way of escape had been provided. Where does one begin? Right at the beginning. He opened his Bible and read: "In the beginning God . . ." and went from there. Each Sunday when the Amen had been said at the village service, he'd head back to these bush people with a further message from God's Word. Each week he covered the same material, yet adding a little bit more—creation, sin, condemnation, promise, Ten Commandments, and finally the fulfillment of that promise of a Deliverer from sin in the person of the Lord Jesus Christ, God's only Son.

At last the morning came. For several months now they had listened, and the Holy Spirit brought it clear to their understanding. "Who is willing to walk the path of this One who loves you?" he asked. It must be no spur-of-the moment decision. He was asking them to exchange their spirit-possessed objects for

130

an invisible, powerful God, One they would accept and follow by faith alone.

The old chief knelt first, then the Little Old Lady with the Twinkly Eyes, another woman with a small baby, some grown men—14 in all—knelt there in the dust to become the first Lobi adult Christians, and the first woman.

You should have seen the missionary as he pedaled back to the house that morning. You would have thought he'd come into his inheritance! Just a year before the Little Old Lady with the Twinkly Eyes had said, "I have heard the way of God. Now will you come and tell my people?" And the Word confirms that "they that know thy name will put their trust in thee" (Psalm 9:10).

In his medical work as well as in the evangelistic and teaching ministry, he found himself thrust more and more into the demands of another culture. It meant adjusting his ideas and expectations to the ways and values of his people. He didn't try to identify with them outwardly because he didn't feel identification was achieved by wearing a loin cloth, eating rats, or living in a mud hut. What he felt really counted was to have a mind that understands, hands to help others in their suffering, and a heart which responds to their emotions.

Entering into another culture meant recognition of our differences. Anyone has the mentality of a child in matters foreign to his culture.

We were ignorant of their customs and made many *faux pas*. We gave the wrong greetings, failed to offer the required gift, or did not follow social protocol. The doctor knew how to fix a leaky faucet, but he couldn't make a bow and arrow or manufacture the poison to render the arrow deadly. Likewise they were ignorant of many things in our culture. This did not mean one was inferior to the other; we were just different. A mutual agreement was established among them: "You're different from me, but I accept you as you are. I'm different from you, so please accept me as I am."

While the medical work took a lion's share of his time, it was by no means the most enjoyable aspect of his missionary career. He's a teacher and preacher first and then a doctor. He tried to keep this perspective even though surrounded by sick folks day and night.

On Thursday afternoons the boys came for a Bible study in the brush arbor type structure. Sunday was a special day when he laid aside his whites and dressed up in a shirt and tie. This specialness caught on and in time, too, these ragamuffins began to wear their market-day clothes to church.

He loved to preach on Sunday morning, but he liked best his class on Sunday evening. The boys had notebooks and he went through Donald Grey Barnhouse's *Teach the Word*, the boys copying the illustrations in their workbooks. Years later he learned at least one boy still treasured this study book. Thank God for the truth of Isaiah 55:10 and 11—His Word does *not* return unto Him void.

For every victory, it seemed there were two disappointments. The doctor encountered a lot of dishonesty living in a pagan society. He met it on every hand—among household help, yard fellows, clinic workers, and even among church members. Once he asked our houseboy (a Lobi), "Kakaraba, is it true that all Lobis are thieves?"

Kakaraba smiled sheepishly, his white pointed teeth glistening, and replied without the slightest hesitation, "Oui, Monsieur."

Before the church building was erected in the village, the waiting room of the clinic was converted into a chapel on Sunday. One evening the doctor stood before a group of Christian boys while teaching the act of kindness shown by David to the son of Jonathan.

Tibounte sat on a back bench, his Bible open in his lap. Apparently remembering a forgotten errand, he carefully laid his Bible on the bench and sauntered outside. Just as casually he reentered a short while later and followed again the lesson of returning good for evil.

The class ended and the boys dispersed their various ways. The missionary closed up the clinic, but where was the key? He was certain he left it in the door. Still puzzled, he walked to the house for a duplicate and then returned to lock up. Now his puzzlement grew for the door was already locked!

There's a solution to every problem, he rationalized, but before he hit on this one, Tibounte walked around the corner.

"Bon soir encore, Tibounte."

"Bon soir, Monsieur."

The boy may have asked a question, but the missionary's mind was diverted by the fact that Tibounte was holding a pair of scissors, scissors that had to come from the bandage room.

"Tibounte, where did you get those scissors?"

"These?" he asked in surprise. "Oh, these! These are just some I brought from home."

LaVerne entered Lobi Land believing that all fine human relationships are built on trust, but trust requires realism. Trust is not the illusion that if you trust him, he'll never do anything wrong.

The pieces of the puzzle began to fall into place. "All right, Tibounte, you say the scissors are yours. But the key is mine, so would you please give it to me?"

"I don't know what you're talking about." He pictured innocence.

"Come with me," the doctor ordered and led the way inside.

Money left in the desk drawer for change was gone. So was the money left at the registration desk. Tibounte followed along like a trusting puppy as the doctor checked first this then that.

A lie to be used must be accepted as truth, and the Lobis are master of this technique. Lying is a weapon, a rhetorical resource just as poisoned arrows are weapons of war and chase. No one caught in a tight corner will forego a good weapon. And Tibounte played his to the hilt that next hour.

At last he broke. "The key is at home," he said tearfully.

The missionary knew it was impossible for him to have gone home in that short time. But he did come over for the *Volkswagen*, and together they drove across town to his house.

Tibounte disappeared into his hut and returned bearing, yes, a key, a clinic key. But it was a missing key to a side door. When this key turned up missing, they began leaving a key in that door and using the back door; thus the stolen key became ineffective.

The missionary almost reached his exasperation point. "All

right, Tibounte. I have no other choice but to take you to Siaka," and headed the car in that direction.

"Siaka?" he echoed. The political chief of town was a man of great power, and his reputation as a disciplinarian was to be feared. Many a thief had his circulation cut off for days because of the tight innertubing wrapped around his wrists.

Tibounte decided to take his chances with the white man. "No, no, Monsieur. Let's go to the mission station. There I will show you everything."

On the other side of the clinic, underneath the kapok tree, Tibounte had hastily hidden his loot—the coins, a syringe, some medicines, and the key.

What Tibounte felt now was a cross between embarrassment and fear-embarrassment at getting caught and fear of punishment. He had suffered plenty under the hands of his own people; perhaps the white man would be more lenient.

"Let's go inside and sit down, Tibounte." Perhaps the lesson he had been immune to publicly might be received if given privately. For the weapon of the missionary was not of physical force but the power of the sword of the Word and the ministry of the Spirit.

It didn't take long for the pastor to realize his words bounced against a solid wall of resistance. Tibounte was genuinely sorry all right, but not because of his sin. He was sorry he had gotten caught.

Trust is the unwavering acceptance of a person as he is, yet it involves always reaching out for the best in him. What parent hasn't taken a child into a store and upon arriving at home finds that child has concealed some unpaid object on his person? Usually after a period of shock and disbelief that *his* child would do such a thing, he gives him a good lecture and embarrasses the child no end by having him return (or pay for) the item with an apology. In such manner he tried to teach the African.

One Sunday following the morning service, the offering plate was brought to the house with a bill missing. This was the first year of the church and each dime could be accounted for! The houseboy and each of us had put in a bill, yet there were only two. Since David brought it, he was chief suspect.

134

Very little goes on in a pagan society without a common knowledge of it. While the doctor deliberated on the matter, David's mother stated that her son had stolen money from the church. Not one to back off from an unpleasant situation, he called David and dealt with him as he would his own child. It never became any easier.

Had there not been those joyous experiences along the way to counteract these sad ones, he might not have been able to bear it.

Koumbolo was a little boy of about ten who had survived tetanus only to be brought to the clinic with a gunshot blast through his leg. The doctor picked out rock, dirt, and debris from three different locations. Recovery was slow because just when he thought it was healing, another rock would work itself out or have to be extracted. Twice a rock worked against an artery, and he almost bled to death before they reached the clinic. The doctor taught them to apply pressure in case of an emergency.

In order to be close at hand, they moved to one of the hospital huts and became a favorite of everyone. His sunny disposition and good humor brightened many a gloomy day. His mother had a new baby and named her Doropo. The first rains of the season were building, and they felt a tug toward home and fields. Dismissal time rested on one wound yet to be healed, and it was progressing well.

Or we thought. On this particular day the doctor drove to our Post Office town for mail, about 45 miles away. Nearly three weeks had passed, and we were eager to hear from the outside world. Since it was our regular sewing class day, I stayed home.

The doctor had hardly driven from the drive when Koumbolo's father came over saying his son's leg was swollen and hard and painful. My old faithful remedy, aspirin, was given with the promise the doctor would look at it the minute he arrived home.

Actually the wound was bleeding inside the sealed up wounds, building up pressure. It reached the exploding point just as I was winding up the class and proceeding to the Bible lesson. "Come quick," Koumbolo's father cried as he raced around the corner of the house. "Blood is spurting everywhere."

135

His mother was following the doctor's previous instructions when I arrived, so we took turns applying pressure. Like she, I knew nothing else to do. It began raining so we crowded inside the circular hut, about a dozen of us. Minutes passed and dragged into an hour. The instant pressure released, the blood gushed forth, once so strong it spurted clear across the hut to the opposite wall.

Then the women lifted their voices in that low mournful wail, a cross between a cry and chant. Had I known how, I might have joined right in with them. Koumbolo, familiar with that chant, knowing it announced impending death, became frightened clean to the core. He raised to a half-sitting position, his black eyes glistening in fear, and whispered, "Am I going to die?"

I looked at my watch. Only a miracle could get the doctor here before another hour. Koumbolo, you're in God's hands. I searched for words to tell him that death is not such a dreaded thing after all. Poor Koumbolo, you've never known anything but pain and discomfort and hunger and want. I didn't know how many other mishaps he had suffered besides tetanus and the gunshot wound. How many headaches, toothaches, earaches, stomachaches? His thin wasted body was mute evidence of knowing hunger. Poverty was his companion. Those scanty, ragged cast off, too big shorts were probably the best clothes he had ever owned.

"Koumbolo, there's something better than living. There's a real place where there's no sickness, no pain, no tears, no sorrow, no hunger, no poverty, and no death. God's Son is preparing this place for all His children, and we become His children by believing He took the punishment for our sin. Yes, Koumbolo, for God's children, there's something better than living."

The motor of the *Volkswagen* seemed amplifed as he drove in the drive. I glanced at my watch and saw the miracle had happened. Seeing the crowd of people thronged about Koumbolo's hut, he stopped immediately, and there stood the tangible expression of an answer to prayer. In no time at all, he had Koumbolo on the table and the bleeders tied off and the leg sewed back. Now, finally, the leg could heal.

136

We never saw Koumbolo again. From time to time someone would come from his village, and he always sent greetings. "He's too busy in the fields to come himself, but he wants you to know he still thinks of you."

Bless you, Koumbolo, you who can neither read nor write or where the gospel is not even preached in your village. May that Word which was sown in your heart grow into real fruition and some day you will experience that for all God's children, there is joy in living.

Over the months many accident victims passed through our doors. People fight with machetes, poisoned arrows, guns, clubs, and knives. Teeth chipped to points make good weapons as well. The people are caught in fires, struck by lightning, attacked by animals, snake bitten, and have fallen from trees. There was no such thing as a normal clinic day. Something happened each day to make it different from all others.

Early in his tropical medical practice, he had thoughtfully and deliberately improvised and made the best of unexpected situations. To be sure, there were times when quick decisions had to be made, yet no one has ever accused the doctor of being impulsive.

One morning an emergency arose in the midst of a heavy clinic schedule. Interrupting an examination, a delegation rushed into the office. "Come into town, quick. A cow has gored Ladji, and his insides are hanging out like—oh, you must quick come see!"

So he did quickly go see. They had spoken true. The cow's horn cut as clean as a surgeon's scalpel. Some people are born with a hernia; Ladji, in his old age, developed one in his lower abdomen in a matter of seconds. His delicate pink organs stood in bold relief to a background of dark skin, dirty clothes, and smelling of filthy barnyard.

In normal circumstances the doctor would never have chosen this surgery, but he wasn't given a choice. The cow made it for him. So in that tiny examining room, surrounded by sweating family and using only an ordinary suture pack, he stuffed those bulging intestines back into the slit and sewed him up. Not until the next day when he watched the patient briskly walk about did the wonder of it all reach him.

Other decisions were not made so easily. One afternoon we made a trip to our Post Office town and drove by the hospital to check on a patient. He almost wished he had stayed in Doropo.

With marked relief, the nurse met him at the door. "You wouldn't want to operate, would you? A man has been here a couple of days with a strangulated hernia. I'm afraid we're going to lose him."

"I thought you sent your surgical patients to Bondoukou. Why haven't you sent him?"

"Can't. The ambulance is broken down."

"Then why don't you send him by taxi?"

"The family has been looking for one all day. None available. You're sure you won't do it?"

But, of course not, and he had perfectly legitimate reasons why not. But somehow he couldn't escape the fact that a man was dying, and he had power to do something about it. For the next hour he tried to make other arrangements. It seemed his conscience wouldn't permit him to try it until all other efforts had failed.

There's nothing like meeting your utter helplessness head-on to make you plunge deeply into the depths of God's strength and wisdom. He needed double portions of both during the next two hours.

They led him into an unfamiliar operating room with only an ordinary table. Even the bugs seemed aware of the drama and swarmed through unscreened windows to participate in the activities. The assistants posed before him for instructions, accustomed to different methods and techniques, using strange instruments and even speaking a foreign language.

Rubber gloves first. The first few pairs he tried, his long fingers poked straight through the rotten rubber. The patient lay prepped before him, and he picked up the scalpel for the first time in almost three years, and for the first time the responsibility rested entirely in his hands. There was no specialist on call in case of a failure somewhere.

"Why is it that there should come to me the thought of someone miles and miles away . . . unless it be a need that I should pray?" God sent out his prayer signals.

From the first the patient sickened of the ether and wretched dangerously. There was no suction tube when he aspirated some of the vomitus or no gastric tube for his distended abdomen.

They survived—both doctor and patient. One hundred miles seemed a great distance to make daily rounds, but he did it—for three days! It wasn't enough to see that he was alive; he was going to see he stayed that way.

Emergencies didn't interrupt only during clinic hours. You could expect them anytime, and especially at mealtimes.

Our lunch was brought to a halt as a noisy procession poured into the clinic yard. This we observed from our dining room table. We hurried over to see the leader carrying a five-gallon paint can and another man carrying a small boy whose head was firmly gripped into the can's narrow opening. Wailing women, concerned family, and curious stragglers brought up the rear.

Blood oozing down his face and around the edge of the can told of the strenuous efforts already exercised to separate head from can. The red blood mixed with the yellow paint powder splotching the black skin reminded one of a halloween mask of a trick or treater.

Boys in Africa are like all boys the world over. Who can say why they stick their heads in a paint can or why they stuff peanuts and corn in their ears or rocks and seeds in their noses? But they do. (So do American boys. Once I was rocking three-year-old Larry and was horrified to find a bean beginning to sprout in his nostril.)

It didn't take an M.D. degree to know the child's head had slipped easily into the can and would likewise come out with no effort if the head were placed in the exact position it went in. And it was done.

"Fer hina foure, fer hina foure," the family gushed their thanks and appreciation.

The fame of the doctor spread. One Sunday afternoon our siesta was interrupted with, "My bucket has dropped into the well," entreated a woman from the village. "Would you come get it out for me?"

Or another time: "Look at the clasp on this case. It's broken. Can you fix it?"

Another: "Our brother has been struck by lightning. Do you have medicine to preserve his body until we reach our village two days journey away?"

"A snake crawled into my fetish house, and we're not allowed to enter. Could you send some medicine to kill it?"

Once someone brought an old portable record player, a relic of a culture not yet known to Lobi Land. "Can you fix it?" they begged. Again the famous doctor worked a miracle and inserted some batteries.

If one can get a small boy's head from a paint can, there seems to be no limit to his abilities.

Our first term on the field was nearing an end. When word got around that we were leaving, people began to wonder. Dan Merkh left the field and never returned. Did that mean that we, too, would not return?

Afia crossed the road and begged us to stay. "Please don't go," she urged. "If you leave, we'll all die."

For these few years the doctor had tried to place himself in the thoughts, feelings, and emotions of another, and it had meant an adjustment in some of his values. He became sympathetic to many of the local ways. He understood why they covered the navel of the newborn, but didn't approve of the cow dung pack covering—there were too many newborns brought with tetanus. So he substituted the sterile dressing instead. He understood why the patients insisted on an injection instead of pills because they had seen miracles follow one single shot. But when their sickness required pills, he'd prescribe a vitamin shot along with the pills—the shot to make them happy and pills to make the doctor happy—and everyone went away happy.

One day at the clinic a Djula woman sat before him in tears. "We've heard you're leaving us," she lowered her eyes. "What will we do without you? You're as a father to us."

This statement surprised the doctor because outwardly there was nothing to relate the two. Yet she had grasped an identification that far surpassed the trappings of food, housing, or

140

clothing. They had experienced the identification of love.

"I'm not leaving you alone," he assured her. "The clinic will be open as usual, and see, Madame Payne has arrived. She is a nurse and she'll take good care of you."

A few months before our departure, the Eddie Payne family arrived in Ivory Coast in time for Sandra to give birth to a sister for four-year-old Laura. Sandra, a registered nurse, took over the clinic in our absence, and the family lived in our house while Eddie built his own just a few yards over to the other side of the property.

Had the doctor realized what an overwhelming task this would be for the new missionary and new mother, he perhaps would have made other arrangements. But apparently the joy of first furlough surpassed realism, and he took off fully persuaded that He who had begun a good work in Lobi Land would continue to do it until we returned.

There's nothing to compare to that first furlough. So much has happened and you can hardly wait to share it with others. You've never been separated so long before from family and friends. Your bones fairly ache to see them all again. An accumulation of four years of heaped-up dreams are right at your fingertips.

We debarked in New York where my parents met us. That afternoon the missionary on furlough stood transfixed in a grocery store before an immense aisle of breakfast cereals. He counted them in disbelief. Forty-nine different kinds! For four years we had only seen oatmeal.

The noise was deafening, especially at bedtime. With an ear attuned to the distant beat of the drum and the soft creak of the katydid, sleep escaped us. And the blaring lights! Don't they even turn them out at bedtime? New York City seemed to be a continual Vanity Fair.

Since both of us were scheduled to speak at the National Association meeting in Raleigh, North Carolina, we needed a crash course in becoming Americanized. The World's Fair was in progress, and that one day there just about did it.

At that first National Association on our first furlough, we felt like divers coming up for fresh air. We embraced those who had so faithfully held the ropes for us. And the singing! Never could we remember such singing. For four years the only music heard on our station was the joyful noises of boys singing translations in unaccustomed keys. Next term we would take a record player and some records, we vowed.

Like a homing pigeon bound for her nest, we headed right back where we left—Memphis, Tennessee. Randall Memorial Church beats with a strong missionary heart. Pastor Norlin Jones, and his people, welcomed their returned family with open arms and a receipt for the first month's rent on a furnished house and filled larder.

The children hadn't suffered from their helter-skelter education. The French system gave them depth, the correspondence method discipline, and from boarding school they encountered competition. This combination put them right at the top of their class as they re-entered the public school system at Messick— Lynn a graduating senior, Lynette a sophomore, and Larry in the seventh grade. That year Lynn starred in the senior play and was awarded the American Legion Award of Honor.

The doctor chose Memphis as our furloughing residence because he felt this a good time to complete the remaining six months of his surgery residence. The board gave their permission with the stipulation that the salary earned be turned into his missions account. This arrangement enabled us to have sufficient funds to return to the field on schedule.

Veteran's Hospital was still located on Getwell Avenue that winter of 1966. Dr. Bowers, chief of surgery, profane yet respectful and helpful, let the resident pick his services. Since we encounter many broken bones in Lobi Land, he elected orthopedics under Dr. Dana, a specialist with Czechoslovakian background. His revolutionary ideas were not fully adopted by the medical profession, not even by his new resident, although he did have to admit, they worked!

It didn't take but a few weeks in America to realize that this was no longer our home. Our home was out there, and just as quickly as we could get the necessary work and travels over, we'd be heading back. As Harry Stam said, we knew we were emotionally ready to return to Lobi Land when we could join in the doxology without crying.

PART IV
THE WORK
TAKES HOLD

---

*He returned refreshed and eager
To pick up where he had left off.
Furlough time was long behind him,
A brand new term lay out before him.
He would do his Father's bidding.
Not just healing, though he touched them
Not just teaching, though he taught them.
He prayed God for understanding
And a turning among the Lobis.*

-15-

Sin In The Camp

Second Term 1966–1970

Since our income had been supplemented from the Veteran's Hospital, our account built up quickly and we were able to return to the field on schedule. Once again we packed our belongings in barrels, shipped them to New Orleans for passage on the *Del Aires*, a freighter bound for Abidjan. Ordinarily, passengers board at the last stateside port, but we were so anxious to get on our way they permitted us to board in New Orleans. They didn't tell us there would be 15 days of stops in Port Charles *and* Houston *and* Mobile *and* Tampa before we at last set sail across the sea. We were tired of the ship before we even left our native land.

Lynette returned with us for her last two years of high school by correspondence, and we three were the only passengers. We had stocked up for hours of leisure time—books, magazines, paint-by-number pictures, games. We had hardly left Tampa before the magazines were dog-eared, the books devoured, the pictures completed, and we were so tired of Rack-O, none of us wanted to hear the name again.

The doctor approached this second term with a good measure of anticipation. Dr. Ruby Griffin, another doctor from Calhoun City, Mississippi, had finished her language study in Switzerland and joined the medical staff in Doropo. This would enable him to get in some formal language study in Lobi for the first six months while she directed the medical work. Too, it was promising to have someone with whom to confer over difficult cases. He had missed this one thing as much as anything in his medical practice.

145

Dr. Griffin's house was still a-building when we reached our station, so she temporarily lived with us. The days passed unhurried as we set up a classroom on the back porch, and each day an informant came to teach us the unwritten Lobi language.

The greatest hindrance to language study is the discipline to stick with it. Interruptions are often seized with the excuse of resting your brains for a minute.

It was in this frame of mind that the doctor received the man who came selling a huge python or boa constrictor. Of course it was dead; they had even severed the head to make sure. White people are always buying all sorts of things, even dead snakes. The doctor justified this purchase by saying its tanned hide would be a catching item on deputation.

It must have been in the midst of learning the plural of certain nouns that the doctor decided to surprise Dr. Ruby when she came home for lunch. Everyone knew this lady doctor was skittish about all sorts of African varmints—lizards, scorpions, even mice, not to mention snakes.

Dr. Ruby usually returned via the back way through the garage, so the doctor arranged the snake just so, half in and half out, giving the impression of crawling into the garage. He seated himself at the table on the porch where with one eye he could see when she left the clinic and the other eye he could see her reaction when she turned the corner. He, however, became very busily engrossed in some paper work. After all, next day he was to give a Bible story in Lobi.

Right on schedule, she turned the corner. "Help!" she screamed and stepped back in terror. Her cries went unheeded to the busy doctor's ears. "It's a nightmare," she thought. Finally "help" did respond, but his smug face told her she was the object of a good joke.

It must have been too good a joke to stop there. I'm not sure which doctor instigated the plan or whether the two hatched it together. The plot moved into motion when darkness descended full on the land. LaVerne tied a string around the neck end of the snake and pulled it across to the clinic, like he pulled his little red wagon in childhood days. He arranged it in the hall with the string going around a corner into the operating room. And waited there in the darkness.

Dr. Griffin called for Guardian, her translator, and asked him to accompany her for rounds in the hospital huts. As they reached the clinic door, she stopped, apparently with a fresh thought. "Oh, I forgot my stethoscope. Would you go in and get it for me please?"

Guardian, wearing loose, unfastened plastic sandals and carrying a feebly lit flashlight (empowered with batteries from our rejects), stepped up and lumbered down the hall. Precisely at that moment, LaVerne tugged the string and the huge python slowly began to crawl down the hall.

In one breath, Guardian dropped his flashlight, dashed back out the door from whence he came, leaving his sandals in their very tracks!

"Quick!" he cried. "Go get Monsieur Payne and tell him to bring his gun. There's a big snake in the clinic," he yelled to whomever would listen.

There are always a raft of children around, so several responded and went across the station to enlist Eddie Payne. Eddie, who is always game for any excitement, loaded his gun and volunteered to save the day. He is also sharp as a tack in detecting the fly in the ointment, and he quickly sized up this situation. The doctors were enjoying this entirely too much for it to be authentic.

Dr. Griffin had barely moved into her new house when Howard and Willie Gage, Pryor, Oklahoma, arrived to build the hospital pavilion. The five hospital huts back of the clinic had served their purpose, but the hospital building would offer so much more—rooms for isolation patients, separate wards for men and women, another office and examining room, bath and rest rooms, and a nurse's station.

Since Dr. Ruby lived alone, the Gages moved in with her, and life on the Doropo station took on a new dimension.

One has to know Brother Gage to appreciate his optimism, sense of humor, and down-to-earth manner of living. You never had to wonder where he was on the eleven-acre station. Just listen. If he's around, you'd hear him whistling.

Mrs. Gage helped with the sewing at DVBS which emerged

into a weekly class. She assisted with entertaining guests, worked for the missionaries, as well as general encouraging and strengthening each of us during their short term.

The day never came when the two doctors practiced together in the medical clinic. The older had barely finished language study when Ruby's father passed away, and she felt the Lord directing her back to the states to care for her aged mother.

It was hard to accept Dr. Griffin's leaving. From the beginning, LaVerne had envisioned a team of doctors at Doropo. Not only would it relieve one of full responsibility and being on call round-the-clock, but a greater outreach could be realized. The outlying areas, especially in the hills northwest, remained virtually untouched. He dreamed of taking a mobile unit in there, say, one day a week, not only to minister to the sick, but to preach the Word as well. But that would mean leaving medical personnel in charge at the Doropo clinic. With Dr. Griffin's coming, his dreams matured into tentative plans.

Once again he faced shattered dreams. His depression was short-lived because he shared something of the comforting presence of the Lord that Abraham felt when Lot separated from him. Hope had not died; dreams were not in vain; they were only postponed. Somewhere, He's raising up another doctor.

So once again he picked up the call of the hills, and his heart strained fervently to respond.

It was among the thorns and thistles of living that he came closest to these to whom God had called him. Shared surpluses often have fleeting values and are perishable. Shared sorrows do not trickle through the fingers so lightly. One day he experienced deep sorrow from four of his most promising preacher boys.

Something vague and menacing brooded in the emerging church, like a festering boil. The missionary is often the last to know of sin in the camp. One spring afternoon the boil came to a head and erupted a putrid spurt of corruption from the lives of four of the fledgling church's leaders.

These four—Benjamin, Jeremie, David, and Joseph—were among those early converts of eight years previously. Now in their late teens and early twenties, unmarried, and untrained, they struggled with spiritual growing pains. What is Christian and what is culture?

Jeremie, a born orator, stood tall, handsome, and as robust as a football star. Friendly, outgoing, yet temperamental and as impetuous as Peter. God frequently visited him in the night. "I wish I knew the Bible well enough to tell my people," he told his pastor one day. "Sometimes I can't sleep for thinking about it."

Remembering his own nocturnal visit from God many years before, the pastor explained that often at night when the world is shut outside, at such a time as this, God is allowed to enter and speak. "It was at such a time as this that God also called me to preach," he told Jeremie.

The pastor arranged for Jeremie to attend a brief term at Bible school. When he returned to his village, he was powerful in word and deed. Until of late, that is. A pagan girl brazenly shared his hut, and he suffered no shame or remorse. He was disciplined and dismissed from the church although he still attended.

"We're praying for you, Jeremie," he was often reminded during those sad days.

Don't be discouraged, O Man of God. Others are faithfully growing in the Lord. Like Joseph, bless his heart.

David was the second to fall into sin. David, tall, slim, muscular, and slightly younger than the other three. He often sulked and his smart-alecky attitude might be chalked up to an inferiority complex. Although his testimony tended to be somewhat wishy-washy, potential welled strong within him. He grew by spurts. More careful guidance and counseling seemed required for David. From time to time a spark exploded revealing a pulsating desire to live a clean, separated life. Lately his growth was encouraging. He itinerated the nearby villages on his own, helped in Scripture translation, and even taught a class in the village church.

One morning in the midst of all this holy activity, he came to the clinic urging the doctor to make a house call to his village. A frightened teenager was ready to deliver his baby.

But look up, dear heart. It's true there was Jeremie and now David, but there are others who are faithful. There's always Joseph.

The doctor ached for Benjamin most of all because more

was expected of him. The only male nurse at the clinic, he worked in close assocation with all the missionary staff. The pastor hoped to see in him what he looked for in his own sons. Short, stocky, winsome, with a mischievous sparkle in his eye that matched his infectious smile, Benjamin was quick, dependable, and of a compassionate nature. His keen intelligence matched a good measure of common sense. His comparatively large salary earned him the Don Juan of the village, with attractive clothes, a bicycle, and a new hut. Girls who had nothing in life to look forward to but babies and a husband beat a steady path to his door.

A lecture of various proportions was often issued with the monthly pay envelope. "Benjamin, you must turn these girls away," the doctor-pastor cautioned. Not only for himself, but the testimony of the church and medical station depended upon it.

"Oui, Monsieur," he answered with his lips, but the lecture might have been given in a foreign tongue for all the effect it had. Not long after, the news filtered to us that a village girl boasted she was carrying Benjamin's child.

The pastor stooped beneath the blow. How much had been expended for such poor results. Were the efforts of the past year to be washed down the drain like so much muddy water? Was there anyone left? Yes, there were a few younger ones coming on with startling possibilities. And oh, yes, don't forget Joseph.

Joseph, the puny one of the lot, could well be named "Rumpelstiltskin" because his skinny, disjointed frame resembled this storybook character. He never had enough to eat and was often sick. Tuberculosis, malnutrition, and amoebic dysentery had ravaged his frail body, but it hadn't diminished his good spirits or refreshing sense of humor.

Joseph's report card indicated a below-average intelligence in school books, but the Holy Spirit quickened his understanding of His Word and gave him a meekness and simplicity of delivery that even the haughty Djula tribe marveled. Joseph came from a village a few miles off the main road, and he hovered over the young Christians there like an old mother hen. Sometimes the strains of "Blessed Assurance" would come wafted on the evening breeze, and we knew that Joseph had assembled the young believers on their logs for evening devotions.

Joseph inspired and encouraged the missionary. That is, until the day when corruption oozed from the lives of Jeremie, David, and Benjamin.

Hard on the heels of their discipline, the pastor caught the drift of a ruffled current. An impetuous Jeremie worded it for everyone. "The pastor thinks Joseph is so righteous. He's just as guilty as the rest of us."

"Jeremie is only chafing under discipline. His words stem from jealousy. Only jealousy. Nothing more." But his words reflected hope more than a statement of fact.

Not one to back off from an unpleasant situation, he called a meeting of his four sons in the Lord. Somehow their future usefulness in the Lord's service seemed weighed in the balance.

He came right to the point. "Joseph, is it true that you are guilty of the same sin for which the others have been disciplined?"

Joseph dropped his head while a stab of fear shot through the pastor's heart. "No," he began. He was not guilty of all that had been said. But yes, there was this one time when he went to take his end-of-the-year examination. This girl had offered herself for the night, but he sent her away. Christians do not act so, he had told her.

Then Joseph had been falsely accused. It had only been temptation, and temptation in itself is not sin, only the yielding to it. But strangely he felt no sense of relief.

Joseph continued. "The night following, the girl returned again." His voice broke and lowered to a whisper as four pairs of eyes gazed as one to catch his next words. "I did not send her away."

"We only have isolated temptations to contend with," thought the pastor. "They have habits of a culture to overcome." Had he possessed their genes and chromosomes, their parents and grandparents, and grew up in their own courtyard, he, too, would see their situation as they did. But he didn't.

Benjamin spoke in defense of all. "Monsieur, I believe the Bible, but some parts of it only work for you white folks. Black men have a stronger sex drive than you." Tragically his limited

Christian experience had never allowed him to meet a sexually pure African.

Since the Bible lay open before them, the pastor turned to 1 Corinthians 10:13 and asked Benjamin to read it. When he finished, he asked, "Benjamin, does that promise specify skin color?"

That day the boys were reintroduced to the One who promised He would never leave or forsake them. One who promised to live inside us and give us the power to do that which we are unable to do of ourselves.

A type of spiritual surgery was performed that day. A habit as natural and instilled as eating was being gouged from their cultural pattern without even a dose of anesthetic to alleviate the pain.

Prayer soothed as a lubricated dressing. The Holy Spirit descended and met with each one and tears flowed freely. Lessons which have been wet down with tears are not easily forgotten. "God forgives and forgets," the pastor told them, "but sometimes scars can disfigure for a long time. We'll have to pray that something beautiful can even come from all this."

They parted and went their separate ways. The pastor trod homeward and collapsed into the first chair. Tears were still moist in his eyes, and his shoulders undeniably drooped. Loving may hurt for a time, but he served a God who specialized in bringing beauty from ashes. And in time, that's exactly what He did in the lives of two of these promising young men.

Not all his sorrow came from the fledgling Christians. The day Larry suffered from a medicine reaction was one of the saddest of his life.

Larry sometimes complained about being the son of a doctor. "You can't even be sick in peace," he grumbled more than once when his father posed over him with a needle and syringe. In his 14th year, however, he faced a crisis which caused him to be eternally grateful his father was a doctor.

A malarial attack had laid Larry low for several days. His fever and headache culminated into a pre-dawn attack of persistent vomiting which resulted in the inevitable injection.

A few hours later before the doctor left to begin regular

clinic hours, he gave Larry a small dosage spansule of the same medication to control the vomiting throughout the day. Most medicines have their side effects, and the doctor knew this anti-emetic was no exception. Periodic checks showed Larry to be listless with no appetite, but apparently free from the symptoms of malaria. "Thank You, Lord, it looks like we have it licked."

That afternoon we knew better.

That Thursday, the women and girls assembled on the back porch for their weekly combination sewing and Bible class. Suddenly the air was shattered by Lynette's blood-curdling cry from within, "Moth-er!" How can such a little girl have such a loud voice?

"What could possibly justify a scream like that," I thought, and rushed through the double doors. Larry framed the doorway of his room, confused, his hands futilely covering the horribly recessed condition of his eyes with the eyeballs struggling to pull deeper into their sockets.

"There's something wrong with my eyes," he whispered in a voice which pleaded, "Help me, oh, please help me!"

The medicine! This must be a reaction to the Compazine. An image of a clinic patient flashed across my vision. After Compazine, she had been unable to control the grotesque spasms of her tongue, just as Larry could not regulate his eyes. *She* got over it. "Please, dear God, let Larry get over it, too."

Lynette raced to the clinic for her father while I led Larry back to bed. Those once beautiful blue-green eyes were so frightening I hid them under a damp wash cloth.

His father had reached him a few minutes later when the spasms began. Like a woman in the throes of birth pains, regular contractions attacked his young body. From somewhere deep inside, these convulsions gradually possessed him, arching his body and threatening to cut off his respiration altogether. Each time his heart seemed more reluctant to pick up the interrupted beat. The doctor strained to strengthen that fragile thread separating life from death.

"I wish I could bear these for you," his father told him once after a particularly severe attack. "Didn't he know he was doing just that?" He suffered each tightening of the muscle and swept along with him through the cycle, never releasing his hold until the limp body sank once again onto the mattress.

Medications to counteract the reaction were given. But when one hour blended into two and two into three . . . and four . . . he was painfully aware that, medically speaking, he could pull up the sheet.

Death was no stranger to him. He wrestled with this Grim Reaper many times those years in Lobi Land. While at times he may appear as a welcome friend, that day he was a haunting specter stretching out clammy claws to claim his own flesh and blood.

Man's extremity is God's opportunity. His loving Heavenly Father, patiently observing the scene, seemed to say, "I'm here. Have you forgotten Me?"

Daddy called for his Bible and read the passage from James 5:14, 15: "Is any sick among you? let him call for the elders of the church; and let them pray over him, anointing him with oil in the name of the Lord: And the prayer of faith shall save the sick, and the Lord shall raise him up." He promised strength in weakness. After almost five and one-half hours, he was weary with his weakness.

The "elders" were sent for—Eddie and Sandra Payne, Howard and Willie Gage, our son Lynn, a student at FWBBC and out for the summer, and Lynette (when she could stay away from the bathroom long enough; this episode, as do all traumatic experiences, upset her gastrointestinal system in the worst way). We knelt around Larry's bed while the doctor anointed his son with the prescribed oil. Brother Gage led us directly to the throne, simply pleading for grace and mercy . . . mercy and grace . . . grace and mercy.

Slowly like oil being poured over troubled waters, a deep calm replaced the suffocating fear. We sensed before we even raised our eyes that the crisis had passed. Larry was asleep and slept peacefully through the night.

Next day as I prepared the noon meal, Larry came bouncing into the kitchen. "I'm all well now," he announced brightly, "so I think I'll go hunting."

154

"Listen. Is that the strains of 'To God be the glory, great things He hath done' that we hear?

"Do we believe all things work together for good? Yes, even good came from this."

On our next furlough, Larry was exposed to the drug scene culture, and peer pressure was great to experiment. But always his father's warning rang in his ears: "Larry, once your body survived a severe drug reaction which may have left you vulnerable to certain drugs. Please be very, very careful what drugs you take. The Lord may not be so merciful next time."

He remembered and took heed.

It was vacation time again. We had a choice between the guest house in Abidjan or occupying a vacant mission house. We had tried the latter, but a missionary is a missionary wherever he is, and a doctor never loses his identity. Even though we were away from the responsibilities of our station, the villagers, unaware of it, just bring new ones. First thing you know, the doctor is conducting a daily clinic with most irregular hours, conducting church services, counseling. Same tasks, different location.

Then we learned of another alternative. France still sailed passenger ships along the West African coast that summer of 1969. We learned that the *General Mangin* picked up passengers in Abidjan, then cut across the equator proceeding directly to Port Noire, Congo. Wanderlust ached in us to see a few of these far away places with the strange sounding names.

A few months before the expected date of departure, the doctor secured passage and made reservations on the *General Mangin* for Lome, Togo, a neighboring French port, about 450 miles away. The fare was calculated—a ridiculously low fare— but the agent explained, "Now, you realize, of course, that the boat does not proceed directly to Lome. You would be obligated to travel with the boat down to the Congo. On the return trip, there would be layovers up to an entire day in port cities of Gabon, Dahomey, and the Cameroons before your debarkation at Lome. You must expect to allow at least ten days for the trip."

What a pity.

For about $5.00 a day we enjoyed the luxury of a French

liner, French cuisine, recreation facilities, maid service, lovely weather, and a smooth sailing since we hugged the shoreline. We spotted another missionary family—they seem to be as common as house dust in Africa—and enjoyed rich fellowship with them.

The doctor became a cheese connoisseur during this trip. France prides herself on her 300 varieties, and he was game to sample them all. Each noon and evening offered a different variety, and he approached each with gusto, even Limburger. At the end of the ten days, he declared Gruyere the winner—from Switzerland, if you please!

Lonnie Sparks, fellow missionary, and his family, drove our *Volkswagen* van to Lome and met us at the boat. We arrived back home enthusiastic to start a new rut that we could leave again in a year.

Sherwood Lee and his family arrived in Ivory Coast during our absence. Sherwood, Vada, and small son Bobby took up residence in the Griffin-Gage house, and once again Doropo blossomed with new life.

Formally untrained, but highly motivated with a great deal of practical experience, Sherwood became the doctor's first assistant in every sense of the word and prepared to take over the medical work when our second furlough came due in a year. This allowed him time to first become proficient in the Lobi language.

We experienced the healing power of the Great Physician many times, and each experience was no less a miracle than the first one.

Afia, another daughter-in-law of chief Bielkhiri, was the 11th patient to be registered at the clinic on that opening day, January 1, 1963. A chronic asthmatic, she had been a regular patient through the years. One needed no stethoscope to chart her irregular breathing punctuated with rattling wheezes. Though never completely free of her discomfort, there were times it was almost unbearable. During these attacks, she would be overcome by a sense of suffocation and pressure in her distended chest, producing unproductive coughs and leaning forward straining to catch hold of her next breath, her dark skin now gray from lack of oxygen.

She was a young girl when he first met her, probably in her

late teens, but she had already borne and buried three children. Often she brought borrowed children to the clinic. He pitied her because an African woman without a child is looked down on with scorn.

Afia attended the sewing classes regularly. Often the other women invited her to church. One Thursday she said vehemently, "I'll come to your class, but I won't come to your church." So it was with great surprise when we saw Afia saunter into church the very next Sunday. Of course, she was topless, barefooted, and no colorful handkerchief covered her close-cropped head. A long cloth reaching almost to her ankles covered her hips and was tucked in at the hips. Regally, like a queen, she glided up the side aisle and squeezed in among the other women crowded there. When the invitation was given, without hesitation, as if it had already been pre-decided, she strode up to the front and knelt at the altar. That morning, Afia renounced the way of the fetish and began a new life by following the true and living God.

Her growth was slow. She was completely illiterate and the only Christian in her village. Sundays often came and went with nothing to remind her that it was the Lord's Day.

Shortly after her conversion, we learned she was expecting her fifth child. The doctor encouraged her to come for regular clinic visits where she was given injections for venereal disease. She relished the yellow vitamin tablets, for they seemed to her a promise of a living child.

In her eighth month she was brought to the clinic in a severe asthma attack which precipitated premature labor. Next morning, the doctor left the waiting room filled with patients and went across the road to help with the delivery of a tiny scrap of humanity weighing less than two and one-half pounds. The doctor carefully wrapped the baby in a cloth under the protest of the family. "Don't concern yourself with that," pointing to the baby. "It's already as good as dead. See that Afia lives."

I met him as he returned wearily from across the road. "Well, Afia has had her baby," he announced and I noted the sadness in his voice.

"Oh, no," I gasped. So it was impossible after all. Afia's shame was not to be lifted. She would never walk among her people with head held high, a child of her own flesh strapped to her back.

The doctor was quick to console, "But the baby is all right," which literally translated meant the baby was still breathing.

Lynette was out visiting that summer from her college days at FWBBC. She walked up about that time and I asked, "Lynette, would you like to have a baby?"

She didn't hesitate one second. She always wanted to take one of these black babies, bathe him, dress him in her doll's clothes, and play with him as a doll. No questions asked, she exclaimed, "Yes!" before I had barely finished asking.

We got a clean towel from the clinic and walked across the road. The baby was still as the doctor had placed her in the lap of a relative. When we asked if we could take the baby, they fairly thrust her at us. We knew she could not survive in those surroundings, and only the Lord could sustain her life in ours. It would be a miracle if she could live, and we accepted the challenge of fanning that flickering spark of life into flame. Lynette named her Suzanne.

Afia was still critically ill. That very night about 2 a.m., a loud wailing penetrated the stillness of the night and interrupted the doctor's sleep. He listened for a few moments, then arose and began dressing.

"Where are you going?"

"To see Afia."

"But they didn't come for you . . . did they?"

"They probably think it's too late."

"Shall I go with you?"

"Not unless I send for you."

His flashlight illuminated a path over the dew-laden trail. The family mutely acknowledged his coming and made way for him to enter the small, circular, windowless hut packed with wailing women. A flickering lantern only intensified the darkness.

"Couldn't they realize they were robbing Afia of the very thing for which she was dying—air?" The doctor had them carry his patient outside where she drank huge gulps of fresh air. They carried her then to the clinic vestibule where the doctor ran a gamut of our available asthma medicine, with a good measure of

158

prayer thrown in. The crisis passed just as the sun stirred in the reddened sky. Suzanne, also hanging tenderly to each irregular heartbeat, endured the night.

The doctor turned wearily toward the house, wondering if it were worthwhile to even go back to bed. Already patients were queuing up before the door to be registered for the new clinic day.

Ten days later Lynette had to return to resume her studies in the States, so Vada Lee took over Suzanne's care during the week. We had her on weekends. When Afia recovered, she came each morning to see how her wee one was progressing. First thing when she entered the house, she'd go to the bathroom and wash well her hands and arms. Then she'd fold this fragile human scrap into her arms. She learned to make her bottle and bathe her. But she didn't want to take her home.

In her third month Suzanne developed a terrible diarrhea which nothing seemed to check. The Lees were on vacation, so we'd take little Suzanne to the clinic with us, and her mother would take care of her in the unused operating room. She weighed less than ten pounds anyway, and ten days of diarrhea had almost sapped every bit of life she had. The day came when she could no longer suck a bottle, and when she cried there was no sound.

"What can we do?" I begged the doctor in desperation. "What would they do if she were in the States?"

The doctor, too, was distressed. He knew her electrolytes were out of balance. "They would test to see what she lacks, and they would supply them in the required amounts." As simple as that.

That day we took Suzanne to the clinic, we told Afia that her baby could no longer suck so she wouldn't need to give her a bottle. Then at noon when we bundled Suzanne to take her home, we knew we had to warn Afia that Suzanne may not be there next morning.

"You tell her," I urged. One could always pass off the distasteful tasks on him.

So the doctor explained that Suzanne was very sick and may not survive the night. I expected Afia to raise her voice in a penetrating wail, but she answered with total silence, almost resignation. But when she leaned over to strap the baby to her back, we noticed glistening in her eyes, tears, small ones. A Lobi woman's tears are many, so they must be small. Troubles are plenty and death often. There are not enough tears to cover all the sorrow. To a woman who had already lost four children, hope was not a thing to be readily clung to.

That night as the rain beat down on the aluminum roof, we gave Suzanne back to the God who had formed her. Perhaps we had wanted her to live so the pagans could see our God was more powerful than the fetish. Perhaps there was a bit of pride or selfishness in that desire. But that night we reached our extremity. "It's bad," I thought, "to die at all, but much worse to die in the rain." Finally, we drifted off into an exhausted sleep.

Early next morning, we were awakened with Afia and her mother-in-law caw-cawing at the door. They came expecting the worst but were relieved to watch the small chest rise and fall in regular breaths. Even we began to hope she might make it.

That afternoon when she cried, there was actually a sound accompanying it. We cut a large hole in one of her nipples, and wonder of wonders, it began to slowly descend down that throat which had been constricted.

All who witnessed this miracle recognized that Suzanne was God's girl, and the fetish had no control over her.

When she was five-months-old and growing normally, the doctor suggested, "Perhaps this is a good time for Afia to take Suzanne home. She needs to grow up in a normal environment."

"But she's still so little yet."

"She'll get so dirty over there."

"It's cold season. Let's wait until warm weather comes."

Wait . . . Wait . . . Wait . . . But finally, we approached Afia with the suggestion. She, torn between desire and fear, at first, refused—"Everyone will want to hold her and they won't have clean hands"—then reluctantly agreed.

By the time Suzanne got too big to strap on her back, the Lord gave Afia another baby daughter, Jeannette. "This God that Afia serves is a powerful one," acknowledged the pagans. "Just look at all those years she followed the fetish, and he never gave her a living child. Now she has two!"

As time for our second furlough neared, the doctor finally decided to forgo further residency training. He chose deputation along with a couple of medical seminars to keep up with new developments in medicine.

No one could possibly enjoy deputation more than this missionary. He loved to visit with the pastors and often served as a sounding board; for they, like most missionaries, are lonely in their responsibility. I used to accuse him of trying to store up enough fellowship to last a whole term.

This furlough we set up housekeeping in my parents' vacant home in Evansville, Indiana. My folks had moved to Southern Illinois to care for my grandmother during her last months here on earth. When the Lord took her home just before Christmas, my family permanently settled in the old home place.

Larry and I were alone much of that year as the head of the house circulated from one coast to the other. He drove 50,000 miles in addition to miles flown. Financially, it was profitable; our account built up sufficiently that we were able to return to the field only a few months past schedule.

Our family underwent radical changes this year. When we deplaned in Nashville, Tennessee, our stateside family met us—Lynn with his wife of a year, Ramona; Lynette was accompanied by her hopeful, Clint Morgan. We rejoiced right away in the wise choices our children had made. Before we returned to Africa, we embraced our first grandchild, Michelle, and LaVerne performed the marriage ceremony for his only daughter at the Cofer's Chapel FWB Church in Nashville.

Not finding a place to call home here in the States, Larry returned to Ivory Coast with us for a year before he enrolled in Hillsdale College, Moore, Oklahoma.

Enroute to our field, we went via Dursley, England. Lister Company, who manufactured our generator, offered to give a free course in maintenance, and even provided room and board. For a whole week, father and son took a motor apart and put it together again. They learned well. A few years later, the generator on the station needed repairs. Father took it apart and son put it back together again.

A church rose up within the village
Her bell summoned loud each Sunday
  Hear the drums beat loud with music
  Hear the swift insistent clapping
  Listen to the Word he preaches
  Bow in prayer, talk to the Father.
These were things he'd long remember
Of his life among the Lobis.

–16–

A Fetish Priest Yields To The Savior

Third Term 1971–1975

The years on the mission field shaped and molded the medical missionary. The picky doctor was not inflexible. He adapted, however reluctantly, to any difficult situation. Look closely though; he no longer chews his fingernails. He dug out the nail clippers and used them regularly. There's something about intimate contact with filth and vermin which discourages nail biting. Dial soap does wonders in removing grime and bacteria but seems most reluctant in removing the taint. It reminded him of his Introduction to Anatomy course that first year in medical school.

He and his partner were assigned a cadaver soaked in formaldehyde. The entire semester they meticulously dissected each vein and organ, nerve and tendon. This class period ended just before lunch. No matter how thoroughly he cleansed his hands, he seemed to get a faint whiff of that preservative every time he put his hand to his mouth.

The doctor always shied away from major surgery. The primary reason was obvious—there was no time. Was he not choosing the better part in caring for the piddling ills of multitudes of people rather than concentrating on a choice few? Even so, in any given day, ordinary patient visits included D&C's, deliveries, suturing, extensive wound debriding, bone-setting, and occasionally Pap Smears, IUD insertions, abscess incisions, etc.

Although major emergency surgery was sometimes obligatory, elective surgery he did not even consider. While the actual

163

hours in the operating room were minimal—one to three hours on an average—the post-operative care was the decisive factor. He had willing and competent-to-a-point African help, yet pitifully untrained. "It takes a nurse to train a nurse," was his motto.

During Sherwood's first furlough he completed his formal nurses training and returned to set up a regular program for training African nurses which greatly relieved the missionary staff.

But when you get right down to it, his reason for postponing surgery was that help was available elsewhere. Undependable. Unpredictable. Often at a great distance. But with the first two objections frustrating his medical practice, this third was a salve to his conscience.

Some patients, such as incarcerated hernias, he loaded into a truck or taxi and sent off with full expectations of a good recovery. Ruptured uteri proved another matter. Of the number ambulanced on for surgery, to his knowledge, not a single one returned alive. Whether enroute, on the table, or an hour or so post-operative, their fate seemed almost predetermined.

Thus these patients could hardly be casually channeled elsewhere. Lonafina came upon the scene shortly after our return from furlough and when Sherwood was well established on the staff personnel.

Christophe, washing the syringes in the injection room and preparing them for sterilization in the autoclave that night when the generator came on, glanced through the louvered windows at the fast-sinking sun. His watch confirmed it to be close to quitting time. He quickened and mentally prepared himself for a refreshing trip into the village.

It so happened he never got to the village. His watch would pass the midnight mark before he left the clinic at all.

At that moment a couple of hurrying messengers left the main road and bicycled right up to the side door. "Oh, oh," thought Christophe as he quickly dried his hands and made his way to the door. Experience had taught him to be prepared for anything and most of it challenging.

The doctor and his assistant, on their way over, met the two men. It didn't take a lot of speculation to recognize the gravity of

164

the situation.

"We live in a village three miles in the bush. Our sister is dying. Our brothers are carrying her to the main road. Will you go after her and bring her here that she may be well?" was the message they delivered.

It seemed that a woman had been unable to give birth naturally, and now the uterus was ruptured and she was bleeding internally. A Caesarean section was all that would save her.

"Sounds like a ruptured uterus, doesn't it, Sherwood?"

"What are you going to do?" There was no doctor at the government hospital and no way to transport the patient on to another 300 miles away.

"What do you think we should do?"

"Let's do it!"

The doctor's assent wasn't given quite as enthusiastically, but he did leave instructions to prepare the operating room while he went for the van to transport the patient. Things like this need mulling over.

That day, or rather night, a different approach to the life and death situation was made. The very modest but air-conditioned operating room was stocked with sterile instruments and supplies, and the make-shift staff prepared to perform a Caesarean section on a patient whose fetus had possibly been dead for several hours.

In retrospect, the doctor says, "To have attempted such a surgical procedure so ill-equipped was almost ridiculous." He had not been trained in OB-GYN (not a likely part of the training in a Veteran's Hospital in 1960); his first assistant had no formal nurses training; his scrub nurse—his 18 year old son—hardly out of high school; and his circulating nurse, his wife, had never even watched an operation.

Man's extremities are God's opportunities, and He certainly took over. A few weeks later, Lonafina walked home to her village and took up her work in the fields. Carried with her was the knowledge that she was a new creature in Christ Jesus because she had personally claimed Him as her own. Later when Joseph the evangelist came to her village, all her neighbors perked up to attention.

The ability to sympathize was easy; they were so pitiful in many ways. To empathize was harder; to enter into another's thoughts, feelings, and emotions could not be gained overnight.

We boil at different degrees. The doctor's boiling point was higher than most men's. He rarely loses his temper and almost never flies off the handle. It seems he has to decide to even become angry. One is quite aware of this deciding process. Tiny lines deepen around his fixed mouth and his jaw muscles tighten sharply, causing his chin dimple to sink like a crater. Crinkles join his arched eyebrows and unite his amber eyes now appearing a shade darker. He bustles about aimlessly, or if at mealtime, he chomps with gusto. Usually he concludes nothing is solved in anger and proceeds from that point.

Since his anger is mild, someone suggested "vexation" as a better word to describe this emotion. Once however, he became "vexed almost to the point of anger."

In the early days it was routine to have various members of the family around while undergoing the treatment. Nothing private about a public courtyard or under a tree. As our facilities increased, the presence of spectators was allowed less and less until it became a rare thing to have family at all admitted with patients.

Once a young and frightened girl needed a vaginal repair following a forceps delivery. She was like a scared deer, so he permitted the girl's mother to remain with her. The mother, so deeply engrossed with the whole procedure, neglected consoling the terrified patient. Once the mother got in the doctor's line of vision, he positioned her elsewhere. She adjusted the sterile towel with her unsterile hands, so he told her firmly, "Do not touch!" The towel got in her way again, so she adjusted it just a little this time, but received a firmer repetition of the previous warning: "Do not touch!" But when she began to pull the skin back to see if the doctor was interfering with an earlier circumcision, he nearly came off his stool!

"No!" he yelled, his dark eyes flashing fire. She jerked back in surprise (or was it fear?). Larry, who was assisting, was just as surprised as anyone and looked up in quick amusement as if to say, "Wow, I didn't know the Old Man had it in him!"

Sherwood can tell about the first time they had a donor for a blood transfusion. A patient with a ruptured uterus had successfully undergone a Caesarean section, but desperately needed blood. Two donors were compatible, so the first lay stretched alongside the patient and preparations were made for the direct method. The doctor would withdraw 10cc of blood, hand it to his assistant who would inject it into the vein of the patient. The needles remained intact although a constant exchange of syringes was taking place.

At least it was supposed to be constant. When the donor saw that second syringe filling up, he decided he'd had it. This pagan society never read the words of Moses, "The life of the flesh is in the blood," but they sense it instinctively. In verity, these vultures were draining his very life from him. "I'm getting out of here, but fast!" he decided and immediately acted on his intention.

The doctor has never knocked down a man, but the temptation welled strong within him at that moment. "Flatten him down on the bed and sit on him if necessary." However, his vexation got him nowhere; the man flatly refused to allow another drop of life to leave his body.

He learned by experience. The next donor stretched alongside the patient, just as had the other. But this time a drape separated him from the action so he was unaware of the draining process.

Once a small amount of blood was drawn from a man for a type and cross match. He was shocked to see this amount drawn and was almost beside himself when he learned it was only a sample, and if his blood matched (it did!) they would want a considerable quantity. He immediately skipped the country and, as far as we know, hasn't been heard of since.

Once a patient was properly typed as a donor; the only catch was his blood was full of wiggly microfilaria worms. The doctor had no choice but to go ahead and transfuse him and later have him return for a filaria treatment.

Often the village vet would come for injectable medicines to treat various humans. The M.D. didn't want the responsibility for this unauthorized medical practice, so one day he kindly suggested the vet stick to animals and leave the humans to him.

One day however, the M.D. invaded the veterinarian's domain.

Merry Mayhew had mixed emotions about their coming furlough. She wanted to see big brothers Jerry and Larry, but how could she leave her cat? Especially now when she was expecting her first kittens. But lovingly entrusting her pet to Aunt Joan Filkins, she took off for America. When these missionaries came to Doropo for a working vacation, the bulging cat came along.

The Medical Center was just the place for a patient unable to deliver, which was the plight of this kitten-sized mama-to-be. The doctor could hardly stand to see anyone in such agony, even an animal. He tched, tched in sympathy and prepared to do a Caesarean.

He seemed to feel an explanation was in order, so he went on record: "I'm doing this as much for Merry as the cat."

Although he maintained a professional relationship with all men of medicine, he had no understanding of the rivalry existing between him and the fetish. Small children laden with charms would be treated without a single rebuke (most of the time) even when the carved images interfered with the stethoscope or dressings. But when the parents would wait three or four days to return a critically ill patient for treatment following the initial visit, he'd be upset.

"Why didn't you bring this child back when his medicine was finished?" Or maybe they hadn't even taken the medicine at all.

A delay of this sort was usually explained with, "But we had to consult the fetish."

Once a child within earshot and eye-range from the clinic died because the fetish refused to give permission to cross the road.

"I do not work with the fetish," he spoke sternly. That the fetish had to approve their visit went against the grain. In time, they did recognize the battle between these two forces, and even the heathen had to admit their fetish was powerless in the presence of the true and living God.

Disoumte was a powerful fetish priest in our area. It signaled his own defeat when he brought his son to the clinic for treatment.

"Look at him? Is he not as a cadaver?" the father spit out the words, trying vainly to hide the acute fear and aching love for his firstborn son. The child was only 11, but he looked like a shrunken old man as he hunched on the bench awaiting his turn for treatment.

Disoumte was ashamed. He who had powerfully entreated for others, had failed to bring health to his own flesh and blood. He had tried, but all he received was silence. Even so, Disoumte continued to raise his two sons in the manner befitting the fetish consultant that he was. They were laden with charms and witchdoctor's magic, but still Idefite had withered and wasted away as the green stalks at the beginning of the dry season.

As usual, when hope died from all other sources, they turned to the white doctor.

"Just look at him. He no longer goes to school. He has no force to work in the fields. He is as the aged." His father spoke sadly as he entreated the doctor for help. Not only the son needs help, the doctor sensed. If only this father, tender over his own son, could know of another Father who also yearned over His Son and His sons yet to be born.

Lab tests revealed Idefite to be suffering from a tropical disease of schistosomiasis (snail fever), a parasitic disease affecting the intestinal tract. The suggested treatment consisted of ten injections give in two-day intervals for a month.

This regular program of treatment enabled Disoumte to hear for the first time in his life the Word of God, One who also had a Son and this Son who loved him and died for him. Every day by tape and spoken word, the message went forth. Had you asked him, "Do you hear what God says to you?" he probably would have answered, "Yes, I hear, but I do not understand."

God in His great love and mercy yearned for Disoumte to understand, so He appeared to him in an unmistakable manner—in a night vision. To his pagan darkened mind, he saw dreams as a means in which secrets, warnings, and the unknown are made known. Disoumte, as all pagans, has a deep respect for the interpretation of dreams.

Disoumte unrolled his grass mat in the corner of his hut, stretched himself upon it, and pulled up a ragged coverlet to his chin. Words he had heard at the clinic echoed through the darkness. "I am the way, the truth and the life. No man comes to the Father except by me."

As he pondered these words, he heard another voice, not an imagined one, but an audible and he called him by name.

"Disoumte, the way of the fetish that you have been following all your life is not the true way. That which you have heard said at the clinic is Truth." Sleep left him the rest of the night. The God whom he had heard of all his life but who was so far away to make contact with, this True One had appeared to him and spoken with him. It was almost beyond belief.

He was so frightened that he lost no time in searching out Joseph, the African evangelist. Oh, the glorious fact of 2 Corinthians 5:17, "If any man be in Christ, he is a new creature." Disoumte's life was transformed from the moment he renounced his old way of life and claimed Christ as Savior and Lord, from the moment he turned his back on the fetish and did a right-about-face on God's way.

Not many Sundays passed before he told his pastor following the morning service, "I have left the fetish. They no longer have power over me. Would you come with me to my house that I might destroy them?"

The doctor will have to stay in Africa a lot longer than he has to fully comprehend just what this involves. To destroy that which has been such an integral part of his life and all those lives he has known; to destroy that which has been so intricately interwoven into every facet of his existence demands divine deliverance.

Although Disoumte had been delivered from the fear of the fetish, the villagers were petrified when they learned of his intentions. They fled their homes in fear lest the wrath of the fetish fall on them all.

The former fetish priest seemed not the least perturbed as he climbed the notched log to the flat roof of his house. A life-size image of a man, molded of clay and poised in a position giving the impression of surveying the village, monopolized the roof top.

170

This idol he called, "The son of God." The blood-streaked idol posed mockingly, a mute testimony of unanswered petitions, the endless sacrifices offered to appease the wrath of Satanic spirits.

Disoumte paused only momentarily beside the clay form, that which had taken so much to be recompensed with so little. Raising his machete high above his head, he clobbered it into big chunks and threw it down piece by piece to the ground below. A god who could be destroyed so easily was no god at all.

Scooping up the dust that remained, he flung it into the air. That finished, he descended the log and stooped to enter the narrow entry to his room and collect the sacred objects harbored there. To the accompaniment of "I Have Decided To Follow Jesus," the mission was accomplished. As the burnable flamed and the indefiable were reduced to uselessness, the radiant smile glowed with the flickering embers. Though clay streaked his sweating body and his home stripped of all he once held dear, a peace sat in his heart that he had never known.

In matter of minutes Disoumte had destroyed one life to begin another. The missionary turned to him and said, "This is no light thing you have done today." Then he challenged. "People have always come to you for consultation, and you have spoken to them with authority. They must be encouraged to continue to come to you. Now you have something to tell them."

The story did not end that morning in the primitive courtyard. It began the ministry of a powerful witness. "He is one of us," the people say and they listen to what he says.

When Disoumte followed the Lord in baptism and came up symbolically risen to a new life, he chose a new name—Paul. Since the church already had a younger Paul, everyone automatically attached "Kontin" to Disoumte's Paul, signifying, "Paul, the aged." In this manner, Disoumte, the fetish priest, became Kontin Paul, preacher of the gospel.

Does it last? Those who are saved from paganism, does it really last?

Kontin Paul as a fetish consultant was a man of comparative wealth with a wife, children, cows, clothing, and a store of cowrie shells hidden under his floor. As a new believer, he was destitute. Forsaken by a wife who chose another man, children in bad health, his cows stolen, money exhausted—he was destitute. (The missionary worried more about his stolen cows than he did. "Those cows aren't mine; they're the Lord's," explained Disoumte with a smile. "He knows where they are.") Yet you never saw a happier man in your life.

Does it really work, you ask? Those who have been converted from paganism? Several years after Kontin Paul's conversion, he had a visitor. He was greeted, given a seat, a gourd of water, and then they got down to business at hand. Opening his money pouch, the visitor handed Kontin Paul a huge sum of money, equivalent to a year's salary for the average laborer.

"I came to you once and asked you to consult your fetish about making me a rich man. You did and today I am a rich man. I want to give this to you as a token of my appreciation."

Was Kontin Paul tempted to take the money? Did he think of all it could buy—clothing for himself and his two sons, a bicycle, perhaps even a motor bike, or even an apprenticeship for his sons? I don't know whether or not he hesitated. But I do know he refused. "That money belongs to the fetish," he told him. "Long ago I left the way of the fetish, so I no longer want to have anything to do with his money."

Unable to read or write, Kontin Paul sits with his open Bible before him, longingly meditating on the words. Perhaps it is in these moments that the Holy Spirit teaches him, for he is possessed of a wisdom that can only come from God.

Just as Disoumte's story did not end in that primitive courtyard, neither did it end with Disoumte's son in the grips of snail fever. After his ten injections, his weight continued to drop and the lab exam showed the continued presence of the disease. Another series of medicines was tried (and failed). Another course, but still lab results were positive.

Once again we had met our extremity, and the doctor was the first to recognize God would have to do it. He told Him so and depositing the boy in the hands of the Great Physician, he took off for vacation.

That first Sunday back at church a young fellow with a big smile came and sat down beside me. Vaguely familiar, he seemed to hold a secret. I glanced and then looked and then frankly stared. It was Idefite! How could one so old and shrunken be so rejuvenated in such a short time? His eyes twinkled, his countenance shone, and he looked almost plump! "Lord, oh, Lord, You really did it, didn't You?"

It was no wonder that a few months later, he too went to Joseph to find the way to God. The two brothers were baptized and took the names of James and Moses.

The years fly by on the mission field, and often vacations were all that broke one year from the other. One night as we were retiring, the doctor asked, "How would you like to forego our vacation this year and go home to the States next fall?"

Never in my wildest dream could I have imagined such a thing! But the thought was so exciting it was as good as planned. "It will be my parents' fiftieth wedding anniversary, and somehow I just feel we should go."

The board had always been sympathetic to the missionary's requests, and they agreed. Details galore were to be worked out, but one by one they fell into place. We had been unhappy about the devaluation of the dollar, but this resulted in a round trip ticket costing less than $600.

We had a delightful visit with our parents and children. We proposed a request to the mission board that any missionary with grandchildren be allowed a two year term. Three-month old Jonathan was now part of our family reunion.

Those August days with his parents were lived to order. His father's weak heart reminded him daily that his heavenly homegoing was imminent, and it suddenly seemed important that things be in order. LaVerne and the other boys, Lynn, Larry, and Clint, repainted the house, outbuildings, and fence. They also cleaned and repaired the property. At last he was content. His house was in order.

The anniversary celebration attracted the whole family clan. That evening gathered around in that tiny living room, our entire family joined together in prayer. A sweet, blessed benediction rested on us.

When he told his father good-bye the following morning, he was unaware that it was his final good-bye and his next meeting would be in a better home above. Ten days later his father departed this land for a heavenly one.

That Sunday morning, having prepared to teach his regular Sunday School class, he was suddenly attacked with a heart seizure which refused to subside. Throughout the day neither devoted family nor family physician could still the summons home. Once he lost consciousness for a few seconds. When he opened his eyes and recognized his loved ones, he asked, "Oh, have I come back?" Was there a slight tinge of disappointment? Had he already caught a glimpse of his Lord?

It was almost ten days later that the telegram reached us in Africa. Robert and Judy Bryan, missionaries in our Post Office town, picked up the telegram on Wednesday afternoon and promptly delivered it to us. Since they usually came on regular mail days, Tuesday or Thursdays, we could not explain this unexpected visit.

"Is this Tuesday or Thursday?" we asked as we jokingly greeted them. "Have we gotten our days mixed up?" Their expression indicated this was no joyful occasion, so we paced ourselves to match their mood.

They handed us the telegram and we read it together. The bereaved son dropped in a chair holding the paper before him, sitting thus for a long while. It took some time to mentally span the 6,000 miles separating him from memories of home. Finally he spoke, "Now I understand why the Lord permitted us to go home when He did."

Fact would not become a reality until furlough when his father would not run out to greet him. But for now, he knew he was where God wanted him, and where both his mother and dad wanted him.

There were no sharp divisions in the four branches of medical practice—medicine, surgery, obstetrics, and pediatrics—in Lobi Land. He was a diagnostician as well as a surgeon, an obstetrician as well as a pediatrician, an internist, gynecologist, orthopedist, dermatologist, urologist, etc. His demand branched into other professions. He was a dentist, nurse, lab and med technician, pharmacist, medical superintendent, and often just plain orderly.

He was a teacher before a doctor, and often the love of teaching surpassed his joy in ministering to the sick. His gift, however, seems to be more in the line of teaching than exhortation. He preaches and teaches the Word and asks the Holy Spirit to make it applicable to each heart. Since the Word is quick and powerful and sharper than any two-edged sword, he figures his duty is only to present it. The Holy Spirit will do the rest.

During a series of Wednesday evenings, he led in a study of 1 Corinthians, a book written to converted pagans. The teaching was especially applicable because their problems were identical to those of our Lobis.

One night he dwelt on 1 Corinthians 6:19, 20: "What? know ye not that your body is the temple of the Holy Ghost . . . and ye are not your own? For ye are bought with a price: therefore glorify God in your body, and in your spirit, which are God's." Medically speaking, he related some of the habits that are harmful to the body, one of which was cigarette smoking.

At the close of the study, Christophe stood with a question, "If cigarette smoking is wrong, is tobacco chewing a sin, too?" It was a well-known fact that several of the leading women in the church indulged profusely. More often than not, the sermon was disrupted while they leaned out and spit through the open window.

The teacher explained that the Bible mentioned neither, but both were unclean habits, and the Bible admonished us to keep our body clean of bad habits.

Christophe persisted by asking another question. "Is someone who chews tobacco to be considered in good fellowship with the church?" Cigarette smoking had been taboo from the beginning.

It seemed the question was completely ignored as he emphasized other sins the Bible specifically condemns, one in particular, overeating. He read the passage, "Put a knife to thy throat, if thou be a man given to appetite" (Proverbs 23:2). A wave of conviction swept over the audience. Since no one dared to cast the first stone, we turned to prayer.

Later, discussing the meeting, I pointed out, "You know,

175

you never really answered Christophe's question."

"I didn't intend to," he answered. There are other ways of answering a question instead of giving a direct response. He wanted the church leaders to depend upon the Holy Spirit for their interpretation and application to life.

In his medical ministry, it was often necessary to perform surgery in order for the human body to function normally. In his spiritual ministry, he likewise was called upon to serve as a cultural surgeon from time to time. Often he observed patterns of culture that were against his recognized standards. How simple if he could decide what should be allowed and what should be tossed out, modified, or substituted.

The Lobi culture resisted all efforts at spring house cleaning where one throws out "that," keeps "this," ignores "the other," and tolerates "a few." He would end up throwing out more than keeping. For example, no drinking, making, or selling their fermented drink! Adultery? No! Polygamy? Toss it out! Premarital sex? Never! Dancing? Out! But with these discarded remnants of life also go their celebrations and rituals connected with birth, adolescence, marriage, harvest, death, and in many cases, their very livelihood. What do they have left? Absolutely nothing, or a way of life foreign to them. Answers are given so easily by those who have never been near the problem.

After Suzanne went home to live with her parents, she became our little girl on Sundays. We'd bring her home with us from church and keep her until that evening. Afia had soaked up a lot of teaching during these months, and one day she requested baptism.

Her husband had long since chased Manakhir from his house, and she had become the village harlot. There were several pluses in Afia's favor: She had been faithful in church attendance. She maintained a good testimony. Noted for her dancing at funerals in the past, she had been a good girl. Everyone said so. "Afia doesn't dance at funerals anymore." And polygamy shouldn't be a problem, but he thought he'd ask just to be sure.

"You're his only wife, aren't you?"

"No," she answered. "When I had both girls to take care of, I told my husband he'd have to bring his other wife home to help me."

"Other wife?" he echoed. It's the first wife that counts, he'd been told; all others are concubines. So let's just chop this extra wife off and get on with baptism.

But, alas, it so happened that the other wife was the first one. His father had bargained for her; the son had worked for her; she had borne his children but had never left her father's house. Afia, on the other hand, had never even been paid for! She had been stolen from her father's house, and since she never produced any living children, she wasn't even worthy of the bridal price.

What does a good surgeon do when he looks at a diseased or malfunctioning member? "Here's an extra leg; let's chop it off?" Of course not. The patient would go into shock and bleed to death. All nerves are attached to the central nervous system. All the veins, arteries, and blood outlets are attached to the main blood supply. That extra member is part of the organized whole. It can be removed, but only after careful planning and delicate surgery.

In a polygamous society, a woman has fewer children, cooks fewer meals, and has lighter domestic obligations. When an only wife has a child, who helps her so she can rest? Who feeds her husband and her other children when she is sick? Who tends her fields, brings water and firewood? Who comforts her in her labor and stops her cries?

No kinsman will take over the duties of another.

People look for little in marriage, almost never companionship.

It wasn't easy to live between two worlds.

Guiding children to adulthood is rough sailing no matter where you live, but living in Africa took our minds from many of the difficulties. Those things that would destroy family life in the States seemed to be absent for the most part. Even when our children grew up and married, Daddy saw that they never got beyond his reach. The lines of communication remained open.

Sometimes his counsel had to be done by letter. Lynn deputated during a period when fuller hair and moustaches were acceptable in some circles, frowned on in others, and totally condemned in others. When he arrived in France as a missionary, this problem of identification hit him full force, for beards were a status symbol of the learned. His father wrote:

"In I Corinthians 9:19-22, I feel that Paul is speaking of his identification with various types of people. If even in appearance—to some measure at least—we can identify with people we are trying to win to the Lord and thus gain greater acceptance with them, I feel it is perfectly legitimate, provided it does not involve that which is definitely contrary to the teaching of God's Word. So if a neat moustache and beard will enable you to gain a better rapport with the French and a better hearing for your witness, I see nothing wrong with it.

"But there is another side of the coin and I try to look at it, too, in my relationship with our people. Most of them are from the South and are slower to change. Perhaps I should have said, they will not change unless they can be certain that it is not wrong. You know as well as I that many are skeptical of longer hair, moustaches, and beards because they associate these things with a godless, rebellious generation of young people. And many want nothing to do with it, and tragically, want nothing to do with these young people many of whom are looking for someone to care and show real love to them.

"But be that as it may, in the circumstances where we find ourselves, if longer hair or a moustache or beard will not really enhance our effectiveness for the Lord, I feel we should respect the wishes of those who support us—yes, even at the expense of personal liberty. I have learned through the years that a missionary is on display, whether he likes it or not, and really, is it too much for us to sacrifice our personal preferences if standing up for them is offensive to our brethren? I think not."

The most peaceful time of the day is around 6 in the evening on the Doropo station. The sun hangs suspended on the horizon, almost in hesitation. The breezes which had built up to near-violent proportions during the day have died down to innocent little ruffles. Wherever people have gone during the day, they are now pulled toward hearth and home as by a giant magnet.

The doctor also turns the key to the side door of the clinic and heads down the lane toward home. He pauses momentarily. It had been a good day. A normal day with its comedies and tragedies and all the in-between cases of diarrhea, malaria, malnutrition, and parasitic infections generously sprinkled with the more tropical diseases and emergencies. Always the emergencies, any hour of the day or night. The key had been turned in the lock, yet he knew full well that the chances of that door remaining locked until the next morning were practically zero.

That's life on the Doropo station. It had always been so. But for the moment at least, he stood amidst a sea of tranquility. A deep serenity lay on his soul. In that moment there wasn't a doctor in the world he would have traded places with. This was the very spot God had led him, and that makes all the difference in the world.

"Go home, doctor. Go. Have a nice evening." The sun had already cast her vote for the darkness.

Body, mind, and soul and spirit
All bowed down so heavy laden
'Til 'twas almost past endurance.
    "Though I love you, I must leave you;
    I crave rest that you can't give me."
So he left them for a season
Left them in the hands of Joseph.

-17-

Fellowship With Two Dimensions

New York City 1975-1976

The years were taking their toll. This last year on the field was the most difficult of his entire life. Malaria and fatigue had ravaged his body almost beyond the point of endurance. He dragged from day to day and just prayed when furlough came he would be able to walk out instead of be carried out.

That last morning as we sat at the breakfast table, he remarked, "I wouldn't stay here another day for $1,000"; or translated read, "If I stayed here another day, I would have no use for $1,000."

Concerning this period, he wrote, "Our real need is personal. Years ago I read a statement issued by the Christian Medical Society concerning the establishment of a medical work on the mission field. It was suggested that there be a minimum of two doctors on the station. I thought it was a good idea but not really a necessity. Now I think I more fully understand the reason for such a statement. Our past four-year term on the mission field was a busy one with the number of patients registered during the first four months of 1975 passing the 10,000 mark. For the past two years we had exceeded 8,000 for the same period. In addition to the work load, I personally had not been in good health since September, 1974."

Joseph had established himself as a faithful leader in the Doropo church. He married a fine Christian girl, and the Lord blessed them with two children. The pastor looked toward this man with high expectations and relied on him more and more during his ill health. When furlough time came, he fully committed the ministry of the church to Joseph with the assurance of his love and prayers.

The doctor could well have heeded the admonition, "Physician, heal thyself!" and he tried. His weary body craved a series of lazy days aboard a ship with nothing to do except sleep, eat, and be away from every trace of responsibility. He sought passage on a boat, but none was available. Perhaps if we get to Europe, we can find one there, he thought. But when we deplaned at Belgium, he was too exhausted to even explore the possibilities.

Well, there's Canada. We were to change planes in Montreal. We would rent a car and drive slowly across the Canadian countryside, perhaps even spend a few days in a country inn. Nothing more than idyllic dreams. A Rotary Convention had tied up all the Montreal hotels, and no car rental agency would rent us a car to take from the country. We had no choice but catch the last plane for New York.

So less than 24 hours after we left Ivory Coast, we were dumped in New York City, totally unprepared to face civilization again. He did have to admit the sight of American currency and the sound of the English language brought a lump to our throats and a tear to our eyes. We were almost ready to chuck it again next morning when we couldn't figure out how the plumbing worked or how to turn on the remote control television.

Little did we know that in just three months, we would be returning to New York to live. How good the Lord is not to reveal the future all at once.

First item on our furlough agenda was Larry's marriage to a girl named Linda. She was all we needed to make our family complete (unless it would be a granddaughter named Lisa). Once again our whole family was reunited; only the Lord knew it would be seven years before we would be together as a family again.

Although the doctor always doted on deputation, he had to

admit the thought of it almost snuffed out whatever stateside enthusiasm he could muster. At that moment, a letter reached him at the Nashville office. Dr. John Frame, chief of tropical medicine at the Columbia University in New York City, offered him an opportunity to attend the school of Public Health and at the same time work with him in his missionary program.

God leads in various ways. At once an intense longing to return to the classroom welled up within him. It came at an opportune time. Already he sensed that the medical work was ready to take a turn in another direction—that of preventive instead of curative. Why treat the same diseases year after year when something might be done to prevent them from having these same diseases? When parents learn to prevent malaria, check diarrhea, and wipe out malnutrition, why the infant death rate could be cut in half. He tingled with the possibilities.

There was a minor hurdle of board approval, but they had always held a long-range view of the medical work. They pointed out that the day for receiving applications had expired. He would apply and if accepted, they would accept it as a directive from the Lord.

Concerning that year in New York, he wrote in one of our prayer letters: "Now, September, 1975, some 20 years later, I have a strange, uncanny feeling that we have walked this path before. For my wife and I are now in New York City, for one reason only: because God has brought us here. Again, in a miraculous way, God has provided that I might get further medical training in the field of public health, the need of which we have seen developing increasingly over the past several years out in Ivory Coast.

"I was offered a fellowship to continue training here at Columbia University worth about $7,000 in school tuition, fees, books, etc. Of course, living expenses are left to us, and here in New York City, that is no small item. But the Lord has supplied a small apartment, for which we are grateful. There is no rug on the floors, no fancy furniture—in fact, I have had to repair much of

183

what is here. At present, there are no drapes or curtains or even shades to the windows. But we are happy for we are learning once again to live by faith."

We traded the African jungle for the concrete jungle of New York City. The only address we knew was the old Christian and Missionary Alliance guest house on 42nd Street right off Times Square, so we secured lodging there until we found an apartment. Prostitutes propositioned right in our doorway. We were glad to finally locate an apartment off 182nd Street, not far from the Washington Bridge.

Gradually the doctor's health was restored. The 16 blocks he walked each day to and from school quickened his step and rejuvenated his blood. He began to feel alive again. Sluggish of mind and spirit at the beginning of the school term, he actually began to compete with those younger students on their own level.

The generation gap was evident at times. The first day in Medical Ethics class he was tempted to ditch the whole program and return to Africa. He had looked forward to this class, but to his surprise, the renowned professor's lecture was laced with profanity, even bordering on the gutter and obscene. He sat there in class and pondered what to do. Withdraw? How would he explain it?

When the class dismissed that first morning, he walked down the hall to the rest room. As he was leaving, the professor entered and in that moment they were totally alone. The professor recognized his student and asked casually, "Well, how did you like the class this morning? Do you think it will be of any help to you?"

Is this the moment for which he had prayed? "I like the class just fine," he began, "but . . . . "

He didn't have to go any further. "I know what you mean," the professor acknowledged. "The language. I'll try to be more careful in the future." He was true to his word. The class turned out to be very profitable, and professor and student developed a mutual respect for each other.

One day the subject of abortion arose. A lady doctor from Rumania gave her elaborate defense of abortion. When she finished, the professor turned to LaVerne and asked, "Do you agree?" upon which he promptly replied, "Not in the least."

After class , the lady made a point to come and speak with the one who disagreed with her. "Yes, I'll have to admit," she said, "that each time I have performed an abortion, I had this small feeling of guilt inside me."

Thus this year offered opportunities to witness as well as opportunities to learn.

The Christian and Missionary Alliance Church on East 68th Street could not have welcomed us more warmly had we been their own. This denomination maintains churches anyway to support their missionary program, so it marched to the same drumbeat as all Bible-believing missionaries.

The Sunday schedule of services began with morning worship at 11 a.m. followed by lunch at the church. Volunteer help did the work with a small fee collected to cover the cost of food. We visited most all the fundamental churches in New York City before finally selecting this one as our "church away from home." My husband still believes it was this food arangement that enticed me—I always enjoyed eating out.

At 1:30 pastor Gene McGee conducted an open forum on his morning message. It was apparent these lively discussions contributed to the spiritual growth and development of his flock.

From 2 to 3 p.m., Sunday School classes resumed. LaVerne was asked to teach the Men's Bible Class. That year he taught Christ according to the Gospel of John to a motley class composed of church officials, new converts, and a surgeon as well as an assortment of men from Project Return, a drug rehabilitation center.

Finally, evening worship came between the hours of three and four. This arrangement allowed for the faint-of-heart to arrive safely from behind the security of their own locked doors before night fall (an important consideration in New York City) while at the same time enjoy the blessings of a full Lord's Day with the saints.

Perhaps the work he enjoyed most that year was his work with Dr. Frame in the actual examinations of missionaries as they returned on furlough. His heart would be forever knit with his kind, and it offered a sense of satisfaction in helping them solve their medical problems. Later that year when we went to live and work at Hephzibah House, we had the privilege of entertaining many of them in this Christian Guest House in the heart of New York City, just a half a block from Central Park in downtown Manhattan.

A missionary is never really weaned away from his people even on furlough. Perhaps the memory is dulled during the day while caught up with the hectic business of living, but at night when all is still, a sound often awakens him in the night and suddenly he is disoriented. Waking, he listens for the crunch of the bicycle tires on the path outside the bedroom window or the wail of the women for the dead or the distant beat of the drum or the call of the katydid. Instead his consciousness absorbs the drone of the airplane, the roar of the fire engine, or the screech of tires on the concrete. Reality hits him like a thud. Before drifting off to sleep , he allows himself the pleasure of remembering Samuel or Jeanette or Paul, and especially Joseph. Realizing God has awakened him for a purpose, he rolls over the side of the bed, onto his knees, and intercedes for these who will always be a part of his life.

It was during these days the telegram reached us: "Joseph gone to be with the Lord." Joseph had already suffered a lifetime of pain in that disease-ridden body. The Lord chose to give him a new body rather than patch up the one he already had.

"Joseph, Joseph, my son Joseph. I would have died for you that the Lobi people be saved. Joseph, Joseph, my son."

When this last furlough ended, we boarded the boat with a greater degree of anticipation than ever before. It was almost furlough in reverse—our children awaited us out there. Lynn and Ramona and their two children were living in one of the three houses on the Doropo station. Clint and Lynette and two little boys would join us in Africa in a year or so following language study. Who said life begins at 40? It was never more promising at 50! His father heart yearned to team up with his children in evangelizing the Lobi people.

Medically it offered a term of challenge. That year in Public Health training permitted him to depart from the traditional in his medical practice, from curative to preventive. For an entire year he had re-thought the principles of medical missions and came up with a strategy that promised to revolutionize medical missions in Lobi Land. Such a move would de-emphasize the medical work as he had practiced it for three terms in favor of a community approach to disease prevention. In other words, instead of treating the same diseases over and over, he hoped to inaugurate a program whereby they would be taught what to do in order to prevent the diseases. When parents learn to prevent malaria, check diarrhea, and wipe out malnutrition, he figured the infant death rate could be cut in half.

During his year in Public Health, he had worked out a program for training paramedical personnel. Choice men would be selected from the outlying villages to come to the medical station to receive basic preventive health care, how to build a latrine, how to purify water, and how to prevent insect bites. Local people would take over the responsibility for their own health instead of depending on American trained personnel in the mission hospital.

Yes, we sensed this term would be different from all others. Just how different, we had not the slightest premonition. Had we known, perhaps we would not have been so eager to board the ship for that fourth term of service.

The Lord allowed us sweet fellowship with another missionary couple before He changed the direction of our lives. Rev. and Mrs. John McKinney, Sr., veteran missionaries to Mali under the

Christian and Missionary Alliance, were returning to their country for a two-fold visit—to celebrate 50 years of marriage as well as 50 years of missionary service. It was not surpirsing to learn that a few months after his arrival on the field, the Lord took him home. I wonder if perhaps this occasion had prompted the visit in the first place.

The doctor asked for special permission to have a Christmas service on ship. The officials graciously granted the request although they didn't participate themselves. A grandmother and her 11 year old grandson joined us. Professing to be Muslims, they seemed to be familiar with the old hymns of the church. The doctor asked about this. "Oh, yes," she replied, "I used to belong to the Methodist church."

And now a Muslim? How could anyone who had come in contact with the Christian faith, know the greatest love story ever told, and then reject it to embrace the Muslim faith? "Would you mind telling me why?" he asked. Her answer blasted a sharp indictment against the Christian church and Christians in particular. "Among the Muslims, I found love. I feel they really care about me. I never found this in the Christian church."

He knew it to be so. Among the Muslims in our village they look after their own, care for them in sickness, feed them when hungry, give them money when broke, and provide jobs. What about Christians? Being converted from paganism, that selfish nature stubbornly rebelled under the process of sanctification. Oh, God, help us produce loving Christians who care.

This third boat trip across the Atlantic lasted only 25 days. The McKinneys debarked at our first stop, Dakar, so we were bereft of Christian fellowship. One January morning we awoke to the sameness of blue expanse of water, same ship's menu, same passengers at their same assigned places at the table, same puzzles and books in the lounge. But there was no sameness about this day, for God spoke to our hearts in such a way that He changed the whole direction of our lives.

"Since we're beginning a new term and a new approach to

medicine, I feel a definite need of God's direction," the doctor began on that decisive morning. "I've been thinking perhaps we should set aside this day as one of fasting and prayer and seek His mind and direction." So he outlined a tentative schedule for the day. We would go our separate ways except periodically we would meet back together for sharing and praying.

That day, as I stood on the deck, looking out across the vast expanse of water, the Lord began to prepare me. "Enjoy yourself," He seemed to say, "you'll never be making this trip again." Was He telling my husband the same thing?

That afternoon as we met again, my husband began almost reluctantly. "I don't know how you feel about this, but the Lord has seemed to impress upon me that this will be our last term in Africa."

I nodded in agreement and then immediately sought to forget it. You can ignore something long enough and it goes away. He'll get back to Africa, he'll become so occupied with the work that he'll forget all about this, I thought. You'd think after 25 years of marriage, I'd have learned better.

So in reality, when we returned to Africa for that last term, it was just to get ready to leave.

He was always teaching, preaching
Stretched out arms were ever reaching
To his people as he met them
Arms to love them and to help them
Guide them, shield them, and protect them
'Til they grew to their full manhood
Patterned after God's own image.
        This love oft he demonstrated
As he lived among the Lobis.

-18-

Au Revoir

That Last Term 1976–1978

We arrived on the field in time for the annual field council meeting in Bondoukou with the entire missionary personnel on hand, including Lynn and his family. A recent demonstration in the village indicated that the stay of the missionary was limited in Africa. Again, the Lord used this to confirm His direction. Whatever we would do, we must do quickly.

In the wake of our arrival, we began to see a raft of measles patients, up to as many as 40 a day. The doctor says he wouldn't recognize this disease as the same he sees in the states. Measles is the second highest killer in Ivory Coast, probably due to malnutrition and poor health habits. Children suffer most. Weakened by the lack of adequate food, they become highly susceptible to a range of deadly diseases, with broncho-pneumonia, gastroenteritis, and eye and ear infections topping the list.

By the next year the clinic staff had mass-vaccinated the whole area, and only two or three cases of measles were treated at the clinic. "This proves it!" he exclaimed. "Preventive measures are the best methods of health care."

The doctor became swept up in the work and the months fairly flew. Although he was contributing to the missionary program, he never got away from those impressions given him by the Lord that day on the ship.

Sometimes we'd go to bed and he'd want to talk about this new thing which loomed before us. Where would we live? There were no ties binding us to any specific geographical location. What would we do? He never aspired to pursue a stateside medical practice. Although he had fond memories of those years at the Bible College, there was no direct communication from there.

Financially it was the worst possible time to leave. After all these years, the board had changed their policy, and now one's salary increased with seniority. Why, we were senior missionaries! Heretofore, Lynn with two children drew a larger salary than the medical doctor.

For the first time in our missionary career, we would be able to save some money. Following that first term, we came home on furlough with a depleted bank account, and only extra gifts from God's people straightened us out. It takes more to operate with teenagers in the house. That second and third term, we almost broke even. Suppose he would stay on another year and save up enough money to set up housekeeping in the states?

Cautiously, I prepared to mention it to him. After all, he, too, was embarrassed that we had no "security" in the states. Once he tried to apologize. "I haven't been fair to you," he began. "Here we are 50 years old, and I haven't provided a home and 'things' for you."

I was quick to assure him that we hadn't needed home and "things." They would only have been a burden. "When the time comes, the Lord will provide what we need." He always had.

I had my arguments all detailed and worked the conversation around to suggest a delay. Not outright disobedience, mind you; even I would never have ventured that. But in the area of postponement. Everyone knows the doctor has a mind of his own, and all final decisions are his. But he does give me the courtesy of listening to my side.

But before I could even word it, he squashed all possibilities with, "If I wasn't so sure the Lord would have us leave, I'd like to stay on for another year."

How then could I even think of suggesting it? So I turned away and mentally prepared to leave on schedule.

Besides one doesn't mope on the Doropo station with so much going on. Life was never as dull as a twice-told tale. Even though he treated scores of mangled hands from exploding homemade guns, each one was different from the others. Once he had five men of various ages from five different villages who had mangled or amputated hands resulting from five different funerals.

No, it seemed one adventure hardly got under way before a new one was tripping over its heels. And always the snakes.

A book about Africa should include accounts of hair-trigger safaris, killers of elephants, and escapades from the lions, buffaloes, and flesh-eating cannibals. Alas, the doctor preferred to capture these animals on film rather than with a gun, to flash them across a screen than display as trophies in his den. He did own a gun, but its use was largely limited to doing away with rabid dogs, snakes and, occasionally, quail.

Africa abounds in snakes. If mongeese are such snake-exterminators, one wondered why they didn't import a truck load of them to our area. In truth, non-poisonous snakes mingled with the potent ones, but the African has a healthy respect for all. We followed suit.

One long ring from the telephone interrupted our dinner. "Monsieur?" Christophe panted from the clinic. "Come quick! There's a snake here in the drawer."

"How do you know it's in the drawer?"

"I saw it, Monsieur. I'm still watching and it hasn't come out."

It was a spitting cobra, he said. He had seen this black serpent with the rose pink belly.

"I'll be right there, Christophe," he promised. These are the doctor's safaris. He padded cotton around his glasses, for these varmints are lauded for 100 percent accuracy up to a distance of 15 feet, and they almost always aim for the eyes. He passed by the garage and armed himself with his trusty machete.

Since dinner was postponed anyway, some of us went along for the sport, maintaining what we figured a safe distance. Next day when we went to the clinic, we saw the snake's dried spittle as thick cream, directed toward the very spot where we were standing, not the doctor.

The Lord gave us a whole year with Lynn and Mona. Mona had a distinct aversion to snakes, partly because her children, Jonathan, 4, and Michelle, 6, played freely on the mission station, and snakes had no respect for property lines.

One day Michelle started to the kitchen door to get a drink. She froze as she spied a spitting cobra also trying to enter. "Mom!" she screamed, "there's a snake here!" Just a few feet away, the snake rose in the air, head swelled, and poised to spit. At that moment, someone, somewhere, prayed. Just as an angel protected Daniel from the jaws of the hungry lions, an angel locked the jaws of that cobra until the yard boy came and killed it. Perhaps that's why Mona detested snakes so.

One Sunday evening we ate dinner with them. Mona remarked, "Well, I told the Lord I'd stay here if He'd keep the snakes and scorpions out of my house." Finding them outside is one thing; inside, another.

That very Tuesday night, about 2 in the morning, the telephone rang. It rang twice before we recognized it. Since we were on a party line system and everyone hears all rings, no one used the phones between ten at night and seven in the morning.

LaVerne grabbed his flashlight and stumbled toward the office. I heard him clearly through the darkness, "A snake? In your house!"

Lynn had gone into the poultry business and brought back a batch of baby chicks. In order to protect them from snakes, he sheltered them in his front-porch office. In the middle of the night, Mona heard a commotion among the chickens, and when she investigated she saw the black snake among a couple of dead chickens.

"Bring the flashlight so I can find my glasses," Lynn yelled in response to her call for help. When they returned, the snake had disappeared. The only thing worse than having a snake in your house is having one and not knowing where it is.

Aided by the Aladdin lamp and two flashlights, father and son searched for a black snake among cartons, bookcases, and furniture. "Watch it, Lynn. This is a spitting cobra," warned his dad.

Finally in a corner behind the desk, their enemy coiled like a charred pastry swirl. Swift blows from a broom handle demolished him.

Lynn stayed long enough in Lobi Land to get the wavering

Doropo church on a solid footing. The pagans wrought havoc after Joseph's death. "See there!" they warned. "Joseph is dead because he preached against the fetish," and implied that would happen to anyone who rejected this unseen god of the underworld. Fear kept many away from church, and those who remained sought to stifle their confusion and doubts.

Lynn organized a committee of elders and met weekly with them for plans, decisions, and church discipline. When Lynn left on furlough, he turned this privilege/responsibility over to his dad. This committee still supervises the Doropo church.

It was a happy day when Mousa became a part of this growing congregation.

No one knew where this old man came from, somewhere up in Upper Volta, he said. He was a foreigner to our area, being claimed by neither the Lobis nor Mossis, although he spoke both languages like a native. Once he embraced the Muslim faith, but they publicly disowned him because he was always too drunk to observe their rituals. Whatever vices the Muslim religion has, drinking alcoholic beverages is not among them.

Mousa guarded the Chain Avion all-purpose store in town. We often suspected the only pay he received to be all the wine he could drink, for old Mousa was almost always obscenely drunk. Two doors enter into this single 12' x 24' place of business; some afternoons when the doctor ran some errands in town, he'd pause to see where Mousa would be and then choose the other door to enter.

Mousa and his old dog shared a lean-to made of a scrap of aluminum roofing slanted against the side of the building. Here he stored his cooking pot and what pitiful belongings he had. He slept on the store's concrete steps.

One afternoon the doctor was called to the side door of the clinic to see a patient the storekeeper had rolled up in a small two-wheeled cart. Heaped inside like a sack of grain was old Mousa. He lay unconscious, feverish, and a quick examination revealed acute pneumonia.

"He won't make it, will he?" the man asked.

"Only the Lord knows that," the doctor replied, "but we'll do what we can."

So he who had been ignored for so long now became a challenge. Perhaps the doctor sought to redeem himself for the way he had neglected this poor, lonely man. He hovered over him day and night until the crisis passed. Mousa and his dog were housed in one of the hospital huts until his strength returned. He couldn't prepare food and had no family to cook for him. No tribe even claimed kinship. So the Christians took over his responsibility, bringing him food and sharing what they had. Gradually his health returned.

One day as Mousa lugged around the walker the doctor had thought would help him in walking, the doctor approached him. "Mousa, the Lord has been good to you. You are well and no longer need medicine from us. You may go now."

Like the Gadarene of old, Mousa begged the doctor not to send him away. Where would he go? Back to the slime pits? We were ignorant of Mousa's background, but we were sure he had experienced something he had never before known—Christian love. We prayed for the day he would come to know the Source of that love.

Mousa began attending the Sunday morning services, first in the Mossi language and then stayed for the second service in Lobi. One morning when we were away on business, Clint brought the message. When the invitation was given, old Mousa left his seat on the back row, walked down the aisle, knelt at the altar, and became a new creation in Christ Jesus.

Like so many of the new Christians in our area, he could neither read nor write. Thank God for the ministry of the Holy Spirit who teaches these helpless ones. He relied heavily on the teachings of others and soaked up this new walk with God.

Albert A. Meiburg gives an illustration to define empathy. He says: "Suppose a person had fallen into the water at the end of a pier and three persons named Pity, Sympathy and Empathy were standing nearby. What would each do? Pity would wring his hands and wail, 'Look, a man is drowning! Someone ought to help him!' Sympathy might plunge bravely into the water, clothes and all, forgetting that he could not swim either! But Empathy would with calmness and forethought secure a rope to the pier and throw it out to the drowning man."

For old Mousa, the doctor had secured a rope and thrown it out to a dying man, both physically and spiritually. By faith, Mousa claimed it. Mousa, a nobody, claimed by no one, that day became a child of the King and heir to all the riches and glories of Heaven.

A deep attachment grew between doctor and patient. Mousa was hired to look after the hospital huts where families of patients lived, in return for his housing and money for food. Each morning as the doctor walked to the clinic, old Mousa would be right there waiting for him. And this hunched gray-haired man is the last person the doctor waved to as he drove out of that drive for the last time.

Several months later, Alice Smith was studying Lobi with Jeannette. They came to the word *bonane*, and Alice asked its meaning.

"That's love," replied Jeannette.

Alice gave her another word which she thought meant love. "It is," Jeannette answered, then explained there are two words for love. "Let me see," she thought, "*Nar* is the love like I have for my husband Samuel. But *bonane*? Well, that's the love like Dr. Miley has for Mousa."

Christmases had always been special on the mission field, and this one would be super-special, for Clint and Lynette and their two boys had arrived on the field. This last Christmas was unlike all the others. Now the spacious house, except for one bedroom, belonged to Lynette, and it was she who supervised plans for that last Christmas dinner in Lobi Land.

"Let's see, Mom," she began. "We thought of having Christmas dinner here this year and having the Paynes, Lees, and Alice. Is that okay?"

"Sounds fine, Sweet. What do you want me to do?"

"Nothing. We've got it all planned. Sandra will bring extra ice from Bouna, Vada said she'd fix chicken and dressing, and Alice will bring tea and green beans."

We were guests and onlookers. Our mental cameras went click, click, click, for we were acutely aware we would never pass this way again in exactly this same way.

That last Sunday morning, the pastor, reluctant to give up

197

his pulpit, chose to preach. Preceding the message, Laura Payne sang a solo, "Jesus Led Me All The Way," and dedicated it to the departing missionary. "Yes, Lord," he thought, "the choice to leave is Thine, not mine. But I choose to follow Thee. One day the words of this song will be my testimony as I stand before Thee face to face."

Ordinarily the church wasn't a gift-giver, but the people wanted to give a part of themselves to their friend before he left them, something purely representative of the Lobi culture. They chose a Lobi bow and a quiver of arrows.

"Every chief has his own bow and quiver hanging in his house as a symbol of his position," Paul explained in his presentation. "You will always be a chief in our eyes."

The missionary's eyes were moist as he accepted the gift, and he knew he would treasure it forever.

That first Lobi service years ago was composed largely of ragamuffin boys. They observed how the doctor exchanged his whites for a shirt and tie on Sunday and gradually sensed that Sunday was a special day. In time they, too, saved their best for this day. Now these ragamuffin boys were well-dressed young men with families of their own. Why, for the first time he was seeing second-generation Christians, he realized, as he watched David beat out his rhythm on the skin-covered drum. Hope swelled in the doctor-pastor's heart as he envisioned their glorious future free from the scars and taint of paganism.

Other mental pictures clicked as we left the church and followed the road about two miles to the *marigot* for our last baptismal service. Old Mousa (and his dog) along with seven others gave witness to the world that they had left the way of the fetish and were beginning a new life in Christ.

A committee from the church had met with Mousa previously to ascertain if he really understood the meaning of this ordinance. "I'm not afraid to die," Mousa testified there on the creek bank. "Now Jesus lives in me and He'll go with me."

Perhaps the memory that will live the longest of those Christmas activities was the skit given by the clinic nurses. Robert Burns, the old Scottish poet, once wrote, "O wad some power the giftee gie us, to see ourselves as others see us."

Perhaps we really do not know ourselves until we see ourselves in that manner. That morning the doctor got a good look at himself through the eyes of his nurses.

If we ever doubted the Africans were born dramatists, those doubts would have been silenced as we observed how quickly the stage was set for the impersonation of the doctor and his wife on an ordinary clinic day.

The front bench was cleared for patients waiting to be treated. A table and two chairs materialized, and Pierre, the doctor, with a stethoscope around his neck and carrying a stack of clinic cards, indicated to the translator that he was ready to see the first patient. After careful examination, Pierre wrote out a prescription and dismissed him down the hall for pills and injections.

While Doc took the blood pressure of a terminally pregnant woman, from the side door a man pushed in carrying his moaning son in pain from a scorpion bite. "Paul, take him please to the injection room and ask Pierre to inject it with novacaine." He calmly dismissed the patient and returned to the anxious woman. She needed lab work.

He walked to "another room" and the telephone. He cranked the handle for one long ring. "Lorene!" he boomed. "Come. I need you," he called in practiced English.

Jeannette (Lorene) had planned to ride my bicycle up the aisle, but when she went for it that morning, it had a flat tire, so second best, she came running from outside and up the aisle to heed the request.

The examination room was a continuous hubbub of interruptions and excitement, but through it all the doctor remained completely calm and unruffled, almost with an air of detachment. Even the obvious offenders were escorted out with careful request.

The most hilarious scene concluded the drama. A patient entered with a huge incarcerated hernia. Kouadjo had inserted a huge rubber ball in his trousers to make it look authentic. The desk became an examining table as the doctor expertly reduced the hernia in plain view of the audience.

Oh, well, privacy was something the Lobis never felt a need of anyway.

We could delay it no longer. A work on the other side of the ocean awaited us. The mission board pays for the cheapest transportation home, usually by plane. Since you are already "there," we have always tried to include some sight-seeing trip enroute back to the States. The only way to remove the sting from leaving, we figured, was to plan some exciting place to visit before we reached America. We explored several possibilities, but finally concluded nothing could be more exciting than Israel.

The news media had made the doctor a very cautious man, so on our next trip to Abidjan, he sought out the Israeli embassy for some assurance. "Why, Israel is safer than your America," the agent told him. "At least we don't have armed men breaking into the mayor's office and shooting him" (which had just been reported from San Francisco).

At last the agent convinced the good doctor, and we booked our flight and made reservations in Christ's Church hostel in Old Jerusalem.

Thus it was, the day after Christmas, we left our beloved Doropo station for that first lap of our journey back to the States. The morning began with all the aspects of a funeral. Finally the last hug, the last prayer, the last tear, and we were on our way.

The doctor allowed himself the luxury of one backward glance. The eleven acres that had seemed so desolate 20 years ago now blossomed with life. Rows of mango and cashew trees, orange and frangi pangi, nerri-pods and flaming flamboyant trees, cacti and crepe myrtle, neatly defined flower beds and clipped lawn bordered by huge stones blended to form a picture he would long remember. Just as he had envisioned that day so long ago, three missionary residences monopolized the far end of the property, a clinic and a 32 bed hospital pavilion flanked the front. A six-unit motel for families of hospital patients had replaced four of the original mud huts.

Lines strung on poles radiated from a generator house from which each evening between 6 and 9:30, the station was empowered with electrical energy. The telephone lines linking each building with the other were strung under the power lines .

He smiled to remember that visitor who asked to use the phone to contact Abidjan, 450 miles away.

A 26 foot water tower crossed his vision, a landmark to those disoriented on the winding paths in the area. So many had contributed to the building of this station—not only in physical labor, but financial support as well. Twenty years before, the Woman's National Auxiliary Convention adopted a $10,000 project to build a medical station in Africa. A recent evaluation by the government estimated it at $175,000!

Good-bye, good-bye. As Clint drove the car out the gate and onto the road, we waved as we went. Strange black faces surrounded him that first day, but now those faces had names and personalities, and he knew many of them as well as he knew his own family. Why, these *were* his family! He had ached with them in suffering, rejoiced with them in good times, birthed their babies, and wept with them in dying. Good-bye. His lips moved in silent prayer.

The car moved slowly down the road for a half a mile and now approached the village. To his left, a white-washed block building with a belfry, green double doors, and green louvre windows gave public testimony of God's work in Lobi Land. For in the midst of his challenging medical practice he never lost sight of that far greater challenge—the challenge of lost souls without Christ. For this he had come. Medicine was God's plan, but it was only a tool to be used in the accomplishment of a far greater task. The church stood as a memorial of what he had helped to accomplish in Lobi Land.

What he had done was far less important than what he had learned. He had seen how the simplest medicine and crudest instruments guided by genuine, tender, and loving care could change superstition and fear into friendship and understanding. They had seen Christianity translated into a tangible, visible thing that they could hold on to and claim for their own.

Yes, it was even as we thought. The anticipated trip to Israel helped remove the sting from the departure. It was a weepy occasion as we boarded the plane. Lynette, who had completed her nurses training in order to return to Africa to help her daddy, sent us off with a note saying all she was unable to. It was like

201

cutting the apron strings in reverse. Daddy's little girl would carry on the work he had begun. Three-year-old Trey wondered, "Who's going to cry for us when we leave?"

To those contemplating medical missionary service, he gives this advice: "To aspire to become a doctor of medicine is a worthy aspiration; to aspire to become a missionary is an even worthier aspiration. To aspire to become a medical missionary surely must be among man's most worthy aspirations. But unless that aspiration has as its source the will of God for one's life, forget it. There are too many obstacles, too many difficulties to overcome without the constant assurance of 'this is the way, walk ye in it' (Isaiah 30:21). But once you have the assurance that God is directing you in this path, don't hesitate. Time is too precious; the course is too long. Just remember: 'Faithful is he that calleth you, who also will do it' (I Thessalonians 5:24). God never calls a person to perform a task without supplying the grace to accomplish it."

A verse which expresses his personal conviction is:

> Only one life
> 'Twill soon be past;
> Only what's done
> For Christ will last.

This is the way he lives.

Epilogue

"He that hath drunk of Africa's fountains will drink again"
—an old Arab proverb

His resignation from the Foreign Missions board became effective August 1, 1979. A few weeks later he participated in the opening activities at Free Will Baptist Bible College where he had been hired as professor of Science and Bible.

For twenty-five years the wheel of his life slowly turned until now it paused at the place of its beginning—Nashville, Tennessee. It seemed his life would forever be interwoven with this institution, either directly or indirectly.

The only activity that surpasses his joy of teaching is his association with the Foreign Mission Fellowship, a student organization geared to encourage prospective missionary students. If in some way he can influence others—younger and better qualified—to replace him on the mission fields of the world, then his leaving Ivory Coast will not have been in vain.

Concerning the future, the former missionary says, "I well remember the joy that my wife and I had even deep in the African bush, for we were following the Lord. And we still experience that same joy and peace, for we feel He has brought us back here."

"Some of our friends have asked us concerning our future plans—do we plan to return to Africa? That is completely in His hands. We simply want to serve Him where He wants us to serve."

Vela Russell
609 West Gum
Walnut Ridge
                    ar 72476

886-6184